MANUSCRIPT SUBMISSION

ABOUT THE AUTHOR

Scott Edelstein has published six other books, including two specifically for writers: *The Indispensable Writer's Guide* (Harper & Row) and *The No-Experience-Necessary Writer's Course* (Scarborough House). Over thirty pieces of his short fiction have appeared in magazines ranging from *Ellery Queen's Mystery Magazine* to *Writer's Yearbook* to *Artlines* to *City Miner,* and he is the editor of the science fiction anthology *Future Pastimes* (Sherbourne Press, 1977).

Edelstein has been publishing his freelance writing since 1972. He has also been a literary agent; a writing consultant; a book, magazine, and newspaper editor; and a writing teacher at several colleges and universities. He lives in Minneapolis.

MANUSCRIPT SUBMISSION

BY

SCOTT EDELSTEIN

CINCINNATI, OHIO

Manuscript Submission. Copyright © 1989 by Scott Edelstein. Printed and bound in the United States of America. All rights reserved. No part of this book may be reproduced in any form or by any electronic or mechanical means including information storage and retrieval systems without permission in writing from the publisher, except by a reviewer, who may quote brief passages in a review. Published by Writer's Digest Books, an imprint of F&W Publications, Inc., 1507 Dana Ave., Cincinnati, Ohio 45207. First edition.

93 92 91 90   5 4 3 2

Library of Congress Cataloging-in-Publication Data

Edelstein, Scott.
    Manuscript submission / Scott Edelstein.
        p.   cm.
    ISBN 0-89879-398-X
    1. Manuscript preparation (Authorship)   I. Title.
PN160.E27   1989   89-39870
808'.02 — dc20   CIP

CONTENTS

WHY YOU NEED THIS BOOK

PART I: ESSENTIAL INFORMATION • 1

1. THE MARKET FOR FICTION • *2*

2. EDITORS VS. AGENTS: MAKING THE RIGHT DECISION • *18*

3. LOCATING THE BEST EDITORS OR AGENTS FOR YOUR WORK • *22*

4. MATTERS OF ETIQUETTE AND FORM • *45*

5. APPROACHING EDITORS • *66*

6. APPROACHING AGENTS • *78*

7. LOOKING YOUR BEST • *88*

8. USING PERSONAL CONTACTS TO SELL YOUR WORK • *104*

9. NOVEL PROPOSALS: WHAT THEY ARE, HOW THEY WORK, AND WHEN TO USE THEM • *113*

Part II: *USEFUL TOOLS* • *120*

10. WRITING SUCCESSFUL COVER AND QUERY LETTERS • *121*

11. THE ART OF WRITING THE NOVEL OUTLINE • *132*

12. ASSEMBLING YOUR NOVEL PROPOSAL • *136*

OUTLINE OF PRISONERS OF PARADISE • *140*

OUTLINE OF TIEBREAKER • *151*

INDEX • *159*

LIST OF SAMPLE
DOCUMENTS

First Page of a Short Prose Manuscript   47
Cover Page for a Book or Book Proposal   48
First Page of Text in a Book or Book Proposal   49
Second Page of a Prose Manuscript   50
Letter Withdrawing a Manuscript from an Editor's Consideration   71
Author Biography Page   94
Page of Excerpts from Reviews   99
Endorsement   102
Cover Letter (Detailed)   123
Cover Letter (Simple)   125
Query Letter   128
Novel Outlines   140-158
  Background/Cast of Characters Pages for *Prisoners of Paradise*   140-141
  Condensed Outline of Opening Chapters of *Prisoners of Paradise*   142-143
  Detailed Outline for Remaining Chapters of *Prisoners of Paradise*   144-150
  Detailed Outline for the Second Half of *Tiebreaker*   151-158

WHY YOU NEED THIS BOOK

Getting your fiction published isn't as simple as it used to be.

For the novelist, things have changed drastically in the past few years. It isn't easy to sell a novel these days, especially if you're a new writer. Many publishers no longer look at unsolicited or unagented novel manuscripts; some no longer consider first novels at all; and a few have stopped publishing novels entirely. It has gotten harder and harder to publish a first novel—and, to a lesser degree, to publish novels in general—over the past fifteen years. It is no longer enough to write a good novel, send it to a publisher you like, and hope it gets published. In F. Scott Fitzgerald's day this simple procedure sometimes led to fortune and fame; today, however, it almost inevitably leads to a cold-shouldered rejection.

Things have changed for the writer of short fiction as well. General-interest magazines that regularly publish good fiction have all but disappeared. The market for short fiction has fractured into several distinct categories: women's magazines, genre magazines (those that publish mystery stories, science fiction, etc.), literary magazines, and so on. At some of these magazines, the door is not as wide open to new writers as it used to be.

Furthermore, whether you are a novelist, a short story writer, or both, you need to know how to carefully research and locate appropriate markets for your work; how to find and contact the right editors and/or agents; how to follow professional etiquette for writers; and how to present your work (and yourself) as positively and professionally as possible. Making and using personal and professional contacts can also make a big difference.

The marketing of your fiction may not be as much fun as the writing, but it's almost as important — and sometimes equally important. You need to be professional in your approach and courageous in the face of rejections.

None of this means that it is impossible to publish good fiction. Every year major publishers in North America release over 2,000 new novels, of which well over 100 are by first-time novelists. Smaller presses issue hundreds of novels each year as well, at least a few dozen of which are by new writers. The novel market is still very much alive; but it is tougher to crack than ever, and the competition is at least as fierce as it has ever been.

The situation for short fiction is similar. For every short story published in North America, magazines and newspapers publish between 100 and 200 pieces of nonfiction. It is virtually impossible to make a living writing nothing but short fiction, and I doubt if there are more than twenty writers living in North America who do it. Yet millions of people continue to read and enjoy short fiction. Hundreds of magazines still publish fiction on a regular basis, and there are now at least half a dozen that publish short fiction exclusively.

As a writer, you of course want to write the best work you can. But nowadays you must also be your own best sales representative. You need to determine which publishers or agents will be most appropriate for your work. You need to understand the standard procedures for contacting and dealing with editors and agents. You must have a thorough understanding of the proper form for manuscripts and letters. And you will be wise to learn how to make use of important contacts in the publishing world to help ensure that your manuscript gets a careful and serious reading.

If you are a novelist, you must know still more. You need to decide whether to submit your novel to publishers directly or have an agent represent it for you. You have to choose whether to send out a completed novel or a novel proposal. And if you write a proposal, you must know how to write the best one possible, so that it makes your book appear intriguing, appealing, and eminently publishable.

Manuscript Submission is the most comprehensive book of its kind. It will tell you everything you need to know on all of these subjects. It will give you clear, specific strategies for keeping your manuscripts out of the "slush pile" and getting them directly into the hands of the right people. It will teach you how to make best use of the writing credits, credentials, and contacts you already have. Most important, it will provide a clear, honest, no-nonsense look at fiction publishing today. In short, it will enable you to give your fiction its best chance for success.

How do I know all this? I've worked as a fiction editor for two book imprints. I've been a writing and publishing consultant since 1980—privately, for a university, and for one of the largest writers' centers in the world. And I know the ideas and suggestions in this book work because I've *seen* them work. With my help in preparing proposals, writing outlines, and composing cover and query letters, clients I've worked with have had their work accepted by major book publishers (including Doubleday, St. Martin's, William Morrow, Putnam, and others), by literary agents (Henry Morrison, Writers House, The Book Peddlers, Arthur Pine Associates, and several more), and by many magazines.

This book will provide you with everything you need to give your work the best chance of being published. It will save you time, effort, and frustration, and help you avoid mistakes and needless rejection. It will help you put your work (and yourself) a step ahead of the pack. And it will help you get your fiction into the hands of the people who can most appreciate it: interested readers.

Scott Edelstein
Minneapolis

PART 1
ESSENTIAL INFORMATION

CHAPTER 1

THE MARKET FOR FICTION

WHEN WRITERS AND EDITORS TALK about fiction "markets," they're referring to organizations and people that publish fiction. There are well over a thousand markets for short fiction in North America alone, as well as several hundred markets for fiction books.

The best-known fiction markets are magazines and book publishers; but many newspapers publish some fiction in their weekend magazine supplements, and at any given time a few dozen editors are busy assembling anthologies of previously unpublished short fiction.

There are other fiction markets as well. Special-interest newsletters and magazines sometimes carry relevant fiction. Some book packagers buy fiction books, acting as middlemen between writers and publishers. Occasionally a press will publish very short fiction on posters or broadsides. TV, film, radio, and stage producers often buy production and performance rights to published novels and short stories.

These markets aren't limited to the U.S. and Canada. There are as many markets of all types, for fiction of all types, outside of North America as there are within it. If you live in the U.S. or Canada, any market in either of the two countries is considered a *domestic* market according to publishing lingo; any market outside the two countries is called a *foreign* market.

Manuscript Submission is not a list of fiction markets; rather, it is a thorough and comprehensive marketing tool. It will show you how to locate the best markets for your work, and how to most professionally and effectively submit what you've written. A comprehensive list of books that *do* list fiction markets begins on page 28.

FICTION IN THE NINETIES

Fiction publishing in North America is alive and well. Thousands of new fiction books, and somewhere near ten thousand pieces of new short fiction, are published in North America each year. A smaller but no less avid audience reads anthologies, short story collections, novellas, and other works of fiction. Libraries continue to spend millions of dollars on new fiction each year.

Nevertheless, the overall market for fiction has changed dramatically in the past fifteen years. Most notably, it has become fragmented into three areas: mainstream fiction, genre fiction, and literary fiction. Each area has its own readership, publications, and general approach. The second of these areas, genre fiction, is itself broken into more specialized markets: mysteries, science fiction, romance, horror, male adventure, fantasy, and westerns. These in turn have still more specialized subcategories, such as heroic fantasy, hardboiled mystery, teen romance, and so on.

Most commercial magazines are quite specialized, targeting their material for a narrow, specific audience. Increasingly, book publishers are taking the same approach, directing both individual volumes and entire lines of books at specific, clearly defined readerships.

Another clear change is that it's harder to break in near the top than it used to be. Nowadays it's *very* tough to publish a short story in a large-circulation magazine unless you've already published a few stories in other reputable publications. It's also more difficult to publish a first novel (except for genre novels) with a major book publisher than it used to be. Indeed, for certain kinds of books, you *must* have an agent to be published by a major publishing house: some presses no longer read unagented manuscripts at all.

At the same time that things are becoming tougher at the top, it is getting easier to break in elsewhere. There are now several hundred literary magazines published in North America, more than ever before. There is also a small but healthy group of literary presses—perhaps seventy in all—that regularly publish books of fiction. Some of these (such as Louisiana State University Press and the University of Pittsburgh Press) are university-affiliated; others (such as McPherson & Co. and New Rivers Press) are independent.

The number of small commercial book publishers is growing steadily as well. Although most of these publish only nonfiction, close to a hundred publish fiction, either solely or in addition to nonfiction. Some of these presses—Mercury House, Soho Press, and Permanent Press, for example—publish a wide range of fiction. Many, however, publish in a single area: religious books, regional books, books for gays or lesbians, etc.

One other area has boomed: genre novels, particularly science fiction, horror, and male adventure. Dozens of books in these genres are published each month.

Another plus is the rise in the number of magazines devoted solely to fiction. Some of these, such as *StoryQuarterly* and *Fiction International*, are literary magazines that have been around for some time. But the 1980s brought us some new magazines— *Story, Modern Short Stories, Stories,* and others—that reach both commercial *and* literary audiences.

An entirely new type of market has also come into being in the past fifteen years: the book packager (also called book producer). Typically, a book packager is part agent and part pubisher: it sells a basic concept for a book to a book publisher, then hires people to write, design, edit, and in some cases typeset the book. Fiction writers can work with book packagers in two ways: by proposing books or series of their own, or by being hired to write a project conceived by the packager or another writer.

A QUICK PUBLISHING GLOSSARY

To discuss the markets for fiction in detail, I first need to define clearly some common publishing terms. These definitions are standard throughout most of the publishing industry; in some cases, however, booksellers and librarians may have their own, somewhat different, definitions.

Adult Books — *Not* books of erotica, but books written primarily or entirely for adult readers.

Category Fiction — Includes romances, westerns, mystery/suspense, male adventure, fantasy, horror, and science fiction. There are also categories within categories, such as sword and sorcery (also called heroic fantasy) and teenage romance. The term is synonymous with *genre fiction*; each of the above areas is called a *genre*.

Children's Books/Magazines — Material for readers ages 5-8.

Clothbound — Same as hardcover.

Genre Fiction — See *Category Fiction*.

House (or *Publishing House*) — A book publishing firm. Occasionally refers to one line, imprint, or division of a large publishing company — e.g., Villard Books (an imprint of Random House).

Juvenile Books/Magazines — *Juveniles* are books for readers ages 17 and under, including young adults (ages 12-17), middle readers (ages 8 — 12), children (ages 5-8), and toddlers (ages 0-5). *Juvenile magazines* are magazines for these same audiences. The terms are synonymous with *young readers* and *junior* (as in *junior books* or *magazines for young readers*).

Literary Magazine/Press — A magazine or book publisher primarily dedicated to publishing good writing, usually fiction and/or poetry, rather than to turning a large profit or reaching a special-interest group. Most such operations are small; some are partially supported by grants and/or educational institutions.

They are differentiated form *commercial* (i.e., "regular") magazines and presses.

Little Magazine — Same as *literary magazine*.

Mainstream — The opposite of *genre* or *category fiction*: fiction intended for a general audience. Occasionally, however, a book that clearly falls into a class of category fiction will be published and promoted as a mainstream book. Examples: Margaret Atwood's *The Handmaid's Tale*; Kurt Vonnegut's *Galapagos*.

Mass-Market Paperbacks — The inexpensive "pocket-size" paperbacks available at drugstores, newsstands, and a wide range of other retail stores, as well as in bookstores. Sometimes called *rack-size* books.

Middle Readers — This refers both to children ages 8-12 and to books and lines of books published for them.

Publishing House — see *House*.

Small Press — Any small-scale publisher. Usually refers to a book publisher that issues 25 or fewer new titles each year. Occasionally used to refer to a literary book publisher.

Trade Paperbacks — Large-size paperbacks sold primarily through bookstores and department stores. They are usually better printed and bound than *mass-market paperbacks*; they are also more expensive.

Young Adults — Readers ages 12 through 17.

THE MARKETS IN DETAIL

What follows is a close look at the major and minor markets for fiction in the 1990s. Of necessity, I'll deal in generalities;

exceptions to any of my points or descriptions are unlikely but possible.

Magazines

Magazines form the largest group of markets for fiction today. Most magazines that publish fiction publish only short stories (up to about 10,000 or 15,000 words), short-short stories (up to 1500 or 2000 words), or both.

The following types of magazines publish fiction on a regular basis:

General-Interest Magazines — Large-circulation magazines, often with international distribution, such as *The New Yorker*, *The Saturday Evening Post*, *Harper's*, *The Atlantic*, etc.

Women's Magazines

Men's Magazines

Genre Magazines — Magazines that specialize in fiction in a single genre, or a set of related genres, such as *Ellery Queen's Mystery Magazine* and *The Magazine of Fantasy and Science Fiction*.

Special-Interest Magazines — Magazines that focus on a single subject or serve a very specific readership, such as *Volleyball Monthly*, *High Times*, and *Senior Life Magazine*. These magazines primarily publish nonfiction, but many of them, including the ones listed above, will publish an occasional freelance fiction piece, provided it clearly relates to the publication's central subject or readership.

Fiction Magazines — Magazines devoted primarily or entirely to short fiction.

Literary Magazines

Regional Magazines — Magazines published for readers living in (or concerned with) a particular city, state, or region.

Religious Magazines

Magazines for Young Readers (ages 12-17)

Children's Magazines (for ages 12 and under)

Newspapers

Most large newspapers publish their own weekly magazine supplements, usually on Sunday (a few publish them on Saturday). Many of these supplements publish fiction, often (though not necessarily) by local or regional writers.

Book Publishers

There are about 150 major publishers of trade books (that is, books for a general audience sold primarily through bookstores and other retail outlets) based in the U.S., and about twenty more based in Canada. Roughly half of these presses publish fiction on a regular basis; about 80 percent of these are open to work by new writers.

There are several hundred much smaller trade publishers in North America that publish 4-25 books per year. About 20 percent — roughly a hundred — of these houses publish fiction titles fairly frequently.

Then there are 200 or so literary presses — small (and sometimes tiny) publishing houses that issue 1-12 titles annually. Several dozen of these regularly publish novels, short story collections, and/or anthologies of new fiction.

Most of the presses that publish short story collections on a regular basis are literary houses. Indeed, unless you are already a well-known or well-published writer, you should look to these presses almost exclusively if you wish to market a collection of your short fiction.

Is it better to try to publish your book with a hardcover house or to go with a paperback firm instead? Today it really doesn't matter. Publishers routinely publish in three formats: hardcover, trade paper, and mass-market paper. A book may be first published in any one (or more than one) of these formats, and it may later be reprinted in any one or more of the others. The same press may publish a book in two or three different formats, and it may sell off reprint rights to another house. Occasionally a paperback press will buy a book, then sell the right to publish a hardcover edition to another publisher. In the 1990s, new writers are published fairly regularly in hardcover, trade paper, and mass-market paper. So don't be concerned with what format(s) a particular press publishes in. Instead, simply look for those presses and editors most likely to be interested in your work.

Book Packagers

Some book packagers work only with a small stable of experienced writers. Others, however, are interested in ideas, proposals, and books from newer writers. Virtually all book packagers are interested in only two types of fiction: series (or individual volumes that will fit into an existing series the packager handles), and heavily illustrated books. Often the packager comes up with an idea, sells it to a publisher, and then seeks a writer to turn that idea into a finished book. Some book packagers handle only adult material; others specialize in books for younger readers; a few handle both.

Typically, a book packager sells a project to a major publisher, then splits the publisher's money with the writer, keeping 25-50 percent for itself. A few unscrupulous packagers try to pay their writers flat one-time fees for their work; you should strongly resist this and insist on at least a 50 percent share of all earnings.

Illustrated Books

It is generally very tough to sell an illustrated fiction book for adults, unless the book is truly special or unusual. The younger the intended audience, however, the easier the selling of an illustrated volume becomes. Children's books—those for ages eight and younger—are almost invariably illustrated; hundreds of such books are published by large and small publishers every year.

Publishers and packagers usually prefer to buy text and artwork for illustrated books separately. That is, they like to purchase only the text from a writer, then hire an artist of their own choice to prepare the illustrations. If the author of a book is not well-known, the publisher or packager will often try to hire a well-known artist to illustrate it, so that consumers and librarians, will buy copies on the strength of the illustrator's name.

Generally, it is best to submit only the text to an illustrated book, unless the artwork you've prepared or arranged for is integral to the text, or so appropriate or dazzling that withholding it seems absurd. If you wish, mention in your cover letter that illustrations are available at the editor's option.

Another effective strategy is to submit only your text without mentioning artwork. Then, when an editor expresses an interest in publishing the book, let him or her know that illustrations are available, and submit a few samples.

Another option you have is to submit the complete text of a book plus two to five sample illustrations. If all the artwork has already been done, say so in your cover letter, and offer to send the remaining illustrations on request. Do make it clear in your letter that the text is available on its own.

If you do submit artwork and text together, the publisher has the right to offer to publish only the text and find an illustrator of its own. However, you in turn have the right to say, "Sorry, but the text and artwork go together; I have to ask you to either take both or return the material."

Anthologies

An *anthology* (or *treasury*) is a book composed of works by several different writers. There are a few regularly published series of anthologies that print new short fiction. Some of these, such as Vintage Press's *The Quarterly* and Penguin's *Granta*, are essentially literary magazines in book form. Some, such as the *Universe* science fiction series, are regular (often annual) volumes of work within a single genre.

More common are one-shot anthologies with a specific theme or focus — stories about horse racing, for example, or fiction by women writers from the midwest. Most anthologies containing new material are open to unsolicited submissions from freelancers, though a few (such as the *New Directions* series) are not. Some foreign publishers, particularly in the United Kingdom, also publish anthologies containing new fiction; these are usually open to submissions from American and Canadian writers.

At least half the anthologies published during any year contain no new work at all, but are best-of-the-year volumes reprinting pieces in a single genre or on a particular theme, or one-shot volumes containing solely reprinted material. Now and then a reprint anthology will be open to submissions of previously published or sold material, but much more often the editor has chosen the complete contents of the book by the time he or she makes a deal with a press to publish it.

There is no single best source for market information on anthology editors who are seeking material. Your most likely sources are the writers' magazines listed on page 28 and, for genre anthologies, newsletters and news magazines that focus on the appropriate genre.

Novellas

A novella is a long story, usually between 20,000 and 40,000 words. It's shorter than a novel but longer than a short story or novelette (a term occasionally used for stories of about 8,000-20,000 words).

Presses that publish books for young adults and middle readers often issue novellas for these age groups as individual books, most often in mass-market paperback. This is probably the largest market for novellas today.

Novellas for adults are published less frequently. Major presses almost never publish novellas in separate volumes unless their authors are quite well known. A handful of small literary presses do publish novellas as books or chapbooks.

A few magazines that regularly publish fiction will publish novellas occasionally, though not often. Genre magazines are the ones most likely to publish a piece of this length. Some literary magazines, particularly those that focus on fiction, also are open to this form. Publishing a novella elsewhere is unlikely.

Excerpted, Serialized, and Condensed Novels

Most publications that print short fiction are happy to publish excerpts from novels, so long as they stand on their own as rewarding and satisfying pieces of writing. Most novel excerpts are 10,000 words or shorter; 15,000 words is usually the upper limit.

The market for serialized and condensed novels has never been very large, but it has shrunk to almost nothing in the past decade. Sometimes a science fiction magazine will publish a novel in two to four parts *if* it is scheduled for publication with a major book publisher. *Reader's Digest* continues regularly to publish condensed versions of books. Outside of these markets, however, magazine serialization or condensation of novels is extremely rare. Furthermore, normally you must first have sold book publication rights to a reputable publisher; usually, in fact, it is the book publisher that arranges the serialization or condensation, not the author or agent.

Newsletters

Newsletters almost never publish fiction, although on rare occasions one might publish a short piece relevant to its subject or audience. For example, a newsletter on cat breeding might run a brief short story dealing with that topic. Since newsletters are often edited and published by one person, it is sometimes possible to persuade a newsletter editor to publish an appropriate fiction piece, even if he or she has never done so before.

Film, TV, Radio, Video, Audio, and Stage

If you're interested in writing material for production, you need to look beyond this book. Here are some good books on writing for these markets:

Writing for film: *The Screenwriter's Handbook*, by Constance Nash and Virginia Oakey (Barnes & Noble).

Writing for television: *Television Writer's Handbook*, by Constance Nash and Virginia Oakey (Barnes & Noble); *Television*

Writing—From Concept to Contract, by Richard A. Blum (Focal Press).

Writing for stage: *How to Write a Play*, by Raymond Hull (Writer's Digest Books); *The Playwright's Handbook*, by Frank Pike and Thomas G. Dunn (Plume Books); *Three Genres*, by Stephen Minot (Prentice-Hall).

Writing for radio/audio: *The Complete Book of Scriptwriting*, by J. Michael Straczynski (Writer's Digest Books).

It *is* possible to sell TV, film, video, radio, audio, or stage production rights to novels, novellas, or short stories without first having to rewrite those pieces into script form. However, with extremely few exceptions, these must be *published* pieces. Furthermore, these rights are almost invariably sold by agents, or by the publishing firms that originally brought the work into print. Selling production rights on your own, unless you know the right people, is just shy of impossible.

Creating Your Own Markets

Although it is a longshot, it is sometimes possible to convince the editor of a publication that doesn't normally publish fiction to publish your work—or even to begin publishing fiction regularly.

The smaller the publication or press is, the better your chances are. Local and regional publications, and one- and two-person publishing operations, are your best bets. Special-interest magazines are also sometimes worth trying, *if* your fiction piece focuses on the same subject as the publication.

Contests

In general, entering more than a very few writing contests each year is a poor use of your professional time and energy. Most writing contests receive between a hundred and several thousand entries, so no matter how good your manuscript may be, the odds are still very heavily against you. There can be only one first-place finisher, and only a handful of winners, and your work will be judged against all the other entries.

If, however, you were to send in your piece as a regular submission, it won't be judged against anything, but will be evaluated on its own merits. A piece that might lose a contest and be returned with a form letter might sell to that same publisher were you to send it in as a normal submission.

To make matters worse, many contests charge entry fees. If you enter multiple contests, this can get expensive very quickly. Your best bet, then, is to enter only those few contests that most intrigue you.

VANITY PUBLISHING

A vanity press is a book publishing firm that makes its money primarily from writers, not from the sale of books. The display ads in writers' magazines and the Yellow Pages that begin "Authors: Manuscripts Wanted" are usually from vanity presses. Typically, were you to submit your work to a vanity press, you'd receive a letter "accepting" your work and offering to publish it. The catch will be that you will have to pay for publication. The cost can vary widely, but a charge of $10,000 to publish a 150-page fiction book is pretty typical.

The big problem with vanity presses is not that they're crooked or incompetent. In fact, vanity presses usually produce well-made, competently designed books, and they almost always live up to every obligation in their publishing contracts. The problem is that vanity presses accept and publish virtually anything that comes their way, so long as authors are willing to foot the publication bill. This means that the quality of vanity press books varies widely. Indeed, most books from vanity houses are downright dreadful. Bookstore owners and managers know this, and therefore stock very few or no books from vanity presses.

Having your work published by a vanity publisher thus may actually *harm* your chances of selling and distributing your writing. Even if you actively hustle your book yourself, you are going to have to overcome bookstores' great reluctance to carry books from vanity houses. Why put yourself in this no-win situation?

Some writers believe, quite mistakenly, that vanity press publication is better than no publication at all. In fact, the opposite is true. Most editors look at vanity press publication as *worse* than no publication, because to them it says that your work isn't strong enough to get published through regular channels, *and* that you're gullible, egotistical, or amateurish enough to pay a vanity press to print it.

SUBSIDY PUBLISHING

Occasionally a book publisher that normally publishes work at its own expense will offer a publishing contract to an author, but ask him or her to pay some or all of the publication costs. Subsidy publishing is a much better arrangement than vanity publishing, because in most cases the publishers have decent reputations among booksellers and librarians, and will do a competent job of designing, publishing, promoting, and selling your book. Normally, you'll receive a royalty on every copy of your book sold, and a portion of any money from subsidiary rights sales; but there's no guarantee that you'll make a profit on your investment, or even that you'll get a significant portion of it back. Subsidy publication is, however, considered a legitimate form of publication by editors, agents, and other publishing types.

Few fiction books are published under a subsidy arrangement. When they are, it is invariably at the publisher's suggestion, not the author's. *Never* suggest a subsidy deal yourself unless you are a friend of the owner of the publishing firm; if you do, your work may be rejected unread, perhaps with a nasty comment.

In general, I advise against accepting a subsidy arrangement. If something is good enough to be published with a subsidy, it is often publishable without one. Suggest to the publisher that it publish your work at its own expense; if the answer is no, try some other publishers.

The only time subsidy publication makes sense is when a manuscript has been very widely rejected, so that you have few other options. Even then, I advise caution; you may be better off revising the manuscript, or letting it sit in a drawer for a year or two, by which time editorial tastes and/or personnel may have changed in your favor.

STAYING SANE

Publishing (and trying to publish) your work are always gambles. *Always.*

This book will provide you with all the information you need to give your work its best chance at publication and success. But no matter how good your work may be or how well you may present it, there is simply no way that you can guarantee publication or success. You can never be sure precisely what editors and publishers will want to publish; indeed, editors and publishers aren't sure themselves. To some extent, publishing decisions are—and always will be—beyond your control.

The wise way to deal with uncertainty is to accept it without worry, anger, or regret. Write the best fiction you can, do the best market research you can, and make your best efforts to sell what you've written. Then let the chips fall where they may. Whatever happens, stay calm and reasonable. Get on with your life—and with your next writing project.

RECOMMENDED RESOURCES

Pages 28-30 of this book list the market resources of most use to fiction writers. Page 26 lists the best resources for researching literary agents. Below are some other books that can be of great help to writers of fiction.

- An excellent book on contract negotiation is Richard Balkin's *A Writer's Guide to Contract Negotiation* (Writer's Digest Books). Also good is Mark L. Levine's *Negotiating a Book Contract* (Moyer Bell).
- A complete, practical, and very useful guide to literary agents is Michael Larsen's *Literary Agents: How to Get and Work with the Right One for You* (Writer's Digest Books).

- A useful and thorough general guide to the business side of writing is my own *The Indispensable Writer's Guide* (Harper & Row).
- The best book on the art of fiction writing is Stephen Minot's *Three Genres* (Prentice-Hall). Good books for beginning writers include Natalie Goldberg's *Writing Down the Bones* (Shambhala) and my own *The No-Experience-Necessary Writer's Course* (Scarborough House).

CHECKLISTS

Major markets for fiction

Magazines:	General-Interest Magazines
	Women's Magazines
	Men's Magazines
	Genre Magazines
	Literary Magazines
	Special-Interest Magazines
	Regional Magazines
	Religious Magazines
	Magazines for Young Readers
	Children's Magazines
	Fiction Magazines
Newspapers:	Magazine Supplements
Books:	Commercial Publishers
	Literary Publishers

Secondary markets for fiction

Anthologies
Book Packagers
Newsletters
Television/Film/Video/Radio/Audio Production
Stage Adaptation

CHAPTER 2

EDITORS VS. AGENTS: MAKING THE RIGHT DECISION

SOME FICTION WRITERS market their work themselves; others have agents handle the marketing end of things for them. Many, believe it or not, do both. Which is best for you?

That depends on several factors: what you wish to publish, where you want to publish it, your previous publications (if any), and whom you know (if anyone) in publishing.

If you wish to publish short work, the answer is simple: market it yourself. Few agents handle shorter material at all—there simply isn't enough money in it. Those few that do take on short fiction normally do so under only two circumstances: 1) if the writer is enough of a literary star to require no more than one or two submissions per piece and to command $1,500 and up per story; or 2) as an occasional favor to writers who regularly produce salable books. Most writers, therefore, must market their shorter work themselves, even if they have agents handling their books for them.

As for short story collections, these are so difficult to sell that few agents represent them. Once again, however, there are some exceptions: 1) if you have a considerable literary reputation; 2) if you have established a reputation in a particular genre and wish to sell a story collection *in that genre*; or 3) if the agent is already representing (or has already sold) at least one of your novels. Even then, no agent will agree to represent a story collection unless he or she feels it has a decent chance of selling to a major publisher.

When it comes to marketing a novel, the issue is far less cut and dried. Your best bet is to have a good agent represent your novel; but no agent at all is better than an agent who is lazy, incompetent, or crooked. A good agent knows hundreds of editors at major publishers, and knows the likes, dislikes, and needs of most of them. He or she keeps on top of the plans, policies, and personnel changes at a wide range of publishing houses. Most important, a good agent knows how to match a manuscript with the right editor at the right publishing house.

A good agent can almost always get you more money and cut you a better deal than you would be able to arrange yourself. Most editors and publishers routinely offer more money and better terms to agented writers from the start.

A submission made by a respected agent will almost always receive a more (sometimes much more) sympathetic reading than one sent in directly by an author—unless the author and editor already know one another. Many editors don't read un-agented submissions at all.

But there are drawbacks to having an agent, too. Most agents tend to deal only with the fifty major fiction publishers. Some agents send their clients' work only to editors they know personally, and thus may overlook some of the most appropriate editors and publishers for certain books. Since most agents have from 10-100 clients each, they won't always make selling your work their top priority. Some won't work terribly hard for writers unless they can command advances of $25,000 or more, and nearly all agents work hardest for those clients who earn them the most money. And of course an agent pockets 10-15 percent (in the case of the sale of certain foreign and subsidiary rights, even more) of the money your book earns.

For most novelists, deciding whether or not to seek an agent boils down to what you want to publish and where you want to publish it.

You'll recall from Chapter 1 the differences between adult books and books for young readers; between mainstream and genre books; and between major and small presses. If you wish to sell an *adult mainstream novel* (or novel proposal) to a major publisher, you have only one real option: get an agent. Without an agent, the odds of selling your book are very close to zero;

indeed, the odds of even getting a careful, serious reading by an editor at a major publisher are very slim. (The one exception here is if you know someone who is a fiction editor or publisher at a major press.)

If you have a *genre novel* (or novel proposal) for adults that you wish to sell to a major press, you do not absolutely need an agent, though you are probably better off with one. Some genre editors (by no means all, but perhaps two-thirds of them) at major publishing houses do read submissions made directly by writers, and buy books directly from writers on a reasonably regular basis. *If* you know your genre well, and have previously published either a book or several short pieces in it, you may do as well or better with your genre novel without an agent. Nevertheless, keep in mind that most genre editors, including those that buy books directly from writers, do most of their buying from agents.

If you wish to sell a *novel, novel proposal,* or *novella for young readers*, or a *book-length story for children*, to a major publishing house, the situation is similar to that for adult genre books. Some editors will consider and buy unagented work, particularly from previously published writers; but if you can get an agent, you are usually better off. These principles hold true for both mainstream and genre books for young readers.

Smaller publishers are an entirely different kettle of fish. The great majority of small presses read unagented material, give that material a reasonably careful reading, and often buy and publish some of it.

Book packagers also can usually be approached without an agent's assistance. Most (though not all) book packagers are perfectly happy to deal directly with authors.

If an agent does take on your work, this doesn't mean that you can count on it getting published. Most good agents sell only 35-50 percent of the projects they represent. The fact is that no one—authors, agents, and even editors themselves—can accurately predict what will sell and what won't. Indeed, of the first seven books I wrote, the only one my agent couldn't sell was the one and only book she was positive she'd be able to place.

CHECKLISTS

Agents regularly represent these forms of fiction:
- Mainstream novels and proposals for adults
- Genre novels and proposals for adults
- Mainstream novels, novel proposals, and novellas for young adults and middle readers
- Genre novels, novel proposals, and novellas for young adults and middle readers
- Fiction books for children

Agents do not normally represent these:
- Short fiction
- Short story collections
- Material appropriate only for small presses, including most literary, university, regional, and religious presses

CHAPTER 3

LOCATING THE BEST EDITORS OR AGENTS FOR YOUR WORK

IT'S QUITE IMPORTANT THAT YOU spend the necessary time selecting editors or agents carefully; a few hours spent doing this careful research can save you weeks of rejection and frustration later.

Let's deal with locating agents first. If you have no need for an agent, expect to do your own market research, and need only to track down the best editors for your work, turn to page 27.

AGENTS

No two agents are alike, and it's important to realize that an agent who may be perfect for one writer may be highly inappropriate, and quite unhelpful, for another. Agents differ widely in their temperaments and styles of doing business. Some are warm and friendly, others curt and businesslike; some are nervous and high-energy, others cool and restrained. Some keep in touch with clients primarily through phone calls, while others prefer to use the mail.

But an agent's personality and style are really secondary considerations. What you need is an agent who is honest and straightforward; who has many contacts at dozens (and ideally hundreds) of publishing houses; who regularly sells fiction books (and, if your project is a genre book, books in that genre) to major publishers; and who will work hard to sell your project. Naturally you want an agent whom you trust, and with whom you get along and feel comfortable; but unless that agent can actually get your project into the hands of the right people *and sell it*, he or she is not doing you much good.

Begin your search for an agent by making use of whatever personal and professional contacts you may have, using the strategies described in Chapter 8. Magazine and book editors in particular can often make excellent suggestions or referrals, particularly if you have a genre book and they edit material in the same genre.

Other writers can also make recommendations. But don't just ask them, "Who's your agent?" Probe a bit. Here are some questions you might ask: "Are you happy with the job she's done for you?" "Does she get your work out quickly, and to at least three editors at a time?" "Does she have a good instinct for finding the right editors for a project?" "Does she stick with a book until she sells it, or does she let it languish if it doesn't sell quickly?" "What are her biggest strengths and weaknesses?"

Ideally, your contacts will be able to recommend at least a couple of agents. Better still, they may also be willing to recommend you and your work to those agents. If you have no useful contacts, however, or if the contacts you have prove less than helpful, there are other effective ways to find good literary agents. One way is to work backward from the projects and writers agents represent. Make a list of some contemporary writers whose work you admire, and/or some recent fiction books you've enjoyed. If your own project is a genre book, list books and writers in that same genre; if your project is for young readers, pick writers and books appropriate for the same age group as your book. *Don't* include bestselling books or writers on this list; the agents who represent Stephen King, James Michener, and Judy Blume are not likely to want to take on new clients, especially little-known ones.

Armed with your list, head for any large city or university library. Begin by collecting authors' names. If you have a title on your list for which you do not know the author, you can usually learn the name by looking up the book in the *Titles* volume of either *Books in Print* or *Paperbound Books in Print*—or, if the book you are looking up is very recent, *Forthcoming Books*.

In Canada, also look at *Canadian Books in Print*.

Next, ask to see the library's biographical dictionaries of living authors. There are quite a few of these; the most common are *Contemporary Authors* (Gale Research), *Directory of American Poets and Fiction Writers* (Poets & Writers, Inc.), *International Authors and Writers Who's Who* (International Biographical Centre/Melrose Press), *Who's Who in U.S. Writers, Editors, and Poets* (December Press), and *The Writers Directory* (St. James Press). For writers of books for children and young adults, also check the multivolume work *Something About the Author* (Gale Research). Listings for many writers also appear in *Who's Who in America* (Marquis) and the regional Who's Whos such as *Who's Who in the Midwest*.

Look up the authors on your list in one or more of these directories. (Some writers will appear in several directories, some in only one or two, some in none.) Each listing will usually include the name and address of the author's agent, if he or she has one. These books should enable you to assemble a short list of agents to contact.

If this search does not lead you to information on all the authors on your list, try calling Poets & Writers, Inc., at 212-226-3586 between the hours of 11 and 3, Eastern time. Poets & Writers has a computer data bank that lists hundreds of fiction writers and, in many cases, the names and addresses of their agents.

Yet another option is to make some quick phone calls to publishers. Let's say you've had no luck tracking down the agent for hypothetical author Susan Wendt. Get a copy of one of her recent books from a bookstore or library. Turn to the copyright page. Look for the name of the original U.S. publisher of the book, and note it down. If no original or previous publisher is listed, you are probably looking at the initial edition, and should note the name and address of the publisher of the edition you're holding.

Writers living in Canada should alter this strategy a bit. See if the copyright page lists either a previous Canadian publisher or a simultaneous American publisher. If a simultaneous American press is listed, this is the firm you will need to call. If a previous Canadian publisher is noted, you'll need to locate a copy of an edition issued by that publisher, then check the copyright page of that edition for the name of the simultaneous American publisher. If no previous Canadian *and* no simultaneous American publisher is listed in an edition, you should contact the publisher of that edition. (If a publisher has both Canadian and U.S. offices, you should normally contact the U.S. office. The one notable exception to this is the paperback house PaperJacks, whose Canadian and U.S. offices operate independently.)

Your next step is to get the phone number of this publisher by calling directory assistance, or by using one of the following directories: *Literary Market Place, Books in Print* (*Publishers* volume), *Paperbound Books in Print* (*Publishers* volume), *Forthcoming Books, Writer's Market, Novel and Short Story Writer's Market*, and/or *Children's Writer's and Illustrator's Market*. Call the publishing house. If the press is small, ask, "Can you tell me the name of the agent who sold you _____ by Susan Wendt?" If the press is large, first ask the operator for the editorial department; then make your request of the person who anwers there. Be patient; it may take a few minutes to get you the information you want, and you may be transferred once or twice. Once you get a name, you can locate the agent's address and phone number in one or more of the books listed on pages 26-27.

The practice of calling publishers for agents' names is neither presumptuous nor unusual, so don't be afraid to do it. If you're asked why you need the information, be honest: explain that you're a writer of book-length material seeking to locate a good agent to represent your work.

Another good way to locate agents is to read the most recent issues (ideally, at least three months) of the magazine *Publishers Weekly*, the trade journal of the book publishing industry. Each issue of *PW* is brimful of the names of agents, editors, and other publishing people. When mentioning agents, *PW* often publishes the names of some of their clients, and/or describes some of the deals they've recently made. The following regular columns will be particularly helpful: Rights, Talk of the Trade, People, and New Ventures.

By now you should have some names, and it's time to head for the reference books. If at this stage you've still come up with nothing, however, don't panic; the reference books will give you plenty of names (though not a great deal of information on each agent) from which to make your selections.

The following books contain good lists of literary agents in North America:

> *Children's Writer's and Illustrator's Market* (published annually; lists many of the agents who handle material for children and young adults)
> *Literary Agents of North America* (published every other year)
> *Literary Market Place* (published annually)
> *Novel and Short Story Writer's Market* (published annually; lists many, though by no means all, of the agents who handle fiction)
> *Writer's Market* (published annually)

These volumes provide names, addresses, phone numbers, and some general information on each agent. Areas of interest and specialization (science fiction, romance, young adult books, etc.), if any, are usually indicated. Agents who handle material for film, TV, and/or stage will usually be coded with a D (for dramatic); these agents of course won't suit your purpose. Agents who handle books will be indicated with an L (for literary). Those who handle both books and dramatic material will be indicated by the letters L-D or D-L.

Some or all of these volumes may be available in your local library; most can be found in any large university library, or in the main branch of any big-city library. These books are usually kept in the reference section, often behind the reference desk. *Literary Agents of North America* and *Literary Market Place* contain the most complete lists of agents; but the other three books provide more information about each agent, including a list of some of the recent projects each agent has sold.

Agents outside of the U.S. and Canada will not be listed in these books; if you are interested in contacting agents overseas, consult one or more of these reference works: *Directory of Publishing, International Literary Market Place*, and *International Writ-*

er's and Artist's Yearbook. These are often available in large libraries.

Keep in mind that bigger is not necessarily better—or worse. There are quite a few one-person literary agencies, quite a few agencies with ten or more agents on staff, and a great many in between. Some agencies of all sizes do a good job; some of all sizes leave a great deal to be desired. In fact, the same agency may have on its staff some excellent and some not-so-excellent agents. What is important is not how large an agency is, but what kind of a job the agent handling *your* work does for you.

MARKET RESEARCH

Most writers need to market at least some of their work themselves. This means that, like it or not, they *must* do their own market research.

This is where some newer writers try to take short-cuts and, as a result, make some of their biggest mistakes. If you send your work to an inappropriate publisher, or even to the wrong editor at the right publisher, you could be utterly wasting your time, effort, and postage. At the very least, your manuscript could end up buried in the "slush pile": those manuscripts earmarked to receive the least, briefest, and least careful consideration. At worst, your manuscript could be returned unread, or even be ignored completely.

Market research is really a two-step process. The first step is determining which markets—that is, which publishers or publications—are right for your work; the second is selecting an appropriate editor at each of those markets.

The *only* way to properly research a magazine or newspaper market is to actually examine at least one recent issue—preferably more. Anything else—listings in resource books and writers' magazines, older issues of the publication, or writers' guidelines—will give you an incomplete, and possibly misleading, portrait of what that newspaper or magazine actually publishes today.

If you have a book project to market, it's just as essential that you find out what sorts of material different publishing houses are currently publishing. Your best and most reliable sources of this information are publishers' own current catalogs; each catalog lists and describes the publishing house's new and forthcoming titles. Not quite as thorough, but still very useful, is the magazine *Publishers Weekly*, particularly the special issues discussed on page 31. Other resources will usually be less thorough or reliable.

I'm not saying that market directories such as *Writer's Market* and magazines and newsletters for writers aren't useful; they most certainly are. But they are places to *begin* your research. Use them to establish an initial pool of market possibilities. You must then research these possibilities more closely and carefully to determine which ones are in fact appropriate for your work.

Following is a list of the most useful market resources for fiction writers. Many are available in libraries, often in the reference section, and sometimes behind the reference desk. I have provided addresses for all magazines and newsletters.

General Markets

Literary Markets — Published bimonthly by Bill Marles, P.O. Drawer 1310, Point Roberts, WA 98281; in Canada, 4340 Coldfall Road, Richmond, BC V7C 1P8

Novel and Short Story Writer's Market — Reference book; published annually in February

Poets & Writers — Published bimonthly at 72 Spring Street, New York, NY 10012

The Writer — Published monthly at 120 Boylston Street, Boston, MA 02116

Writer's Digest — Published monthly at 1507 Dana Avenue, Cincinnati, OH 45207

Writer's Market — Reference book; published annually in September

Writer's Yearbook — Published annually in December by F&W Publications, 1507 Dana Avenue, Cincinnati, OH 45207. Single issues only are available; no subscriptions.

Children's/Young Adult Markets

Children's Writer's and Illustrator's Market — Reference book; published annually in February

Literary Market Place — Reference book; published annually in November. Lists book publishers only

Novel and Short Story Writer's Market — Reference book; published annually in February

Publishers Weekly — Published weekly by Cahners/Bowker, 249 W. 17 Street, New York, NY 10011. Covers book publishing only; consult the special semiannual Children's Books issues

School Library Journal — Published monthly by Cahners, 249 W. 17 Street, New York, NY 10011. Covers book publishing only

Literary Magazines and Presses

Associated Writing Programs Newsletter — Published quarterly by the Associated Writing Programs, Old Dominion University, Norfolk, VA 23529

Directory of Literary Magazines — Reference book; published every other year

International Directory of Little Magazines and Small Presses — Reference book; published annually

Literary Market Place — Reference book; published annually in November. Lists book publishers only

Novel and Short Story Writer's Market — Reference book; published annually in February

Small Press — Published bimonthly at Box 3000, Denville, NJ 07834

Small Press Review — Published monthly by Dustbooks, Box 100, Paradise, CA 95969

Book Publishers

Forthcoming Books (Subject section) — Published bimonthly by R.R. Bowker, 245 W. 17 Street, New York, NY 10011

Library Journal — Published twice monthly (monthly during certain months) by Cahners, 249 W. 17 Street, New York, NY 10011

Literary Market Place — Reference book; published annually in November

Publishers Weekly — Published weekly by Cahners, 249 W. 17 Street, New York, NY 10011

Small Press — Published monthly at Box 3000, Denville, NJ 07834. Particularly useful are its spring and fall Announcements issues, published in April and October.

Book Packagers

Literary Market Place — Reference book; published annually in November. Look under the heading Book Producers.

Foreign Markets

Directory of Publishing — Reference book; published annually. This is a directory of foreign book publishers.

International Directory of Little Magazines and Small Presses — Reference book; published annually

International Literary Market Place — Reference book; published annually. Covers both book and magazine markets, with emphasis on books.

International Writers and Artists Yearbook — Reference book; published annually. Covers book, magazine, and newspaper markets.

Markets Abroad — Published bimonthly by Michael Sedge and Associates, 2460 Lexington Drive, Owasso, MI 48867. Primarily covers periodical markets.

If you have a genre manuscript to market, you should also consult any market resources specific to that genre. For instance, if you're a writer of science fiction, some of your best market resources will be the publications of Science Fiction Writers of America, the professional organization of science fiction writers, and the independent science fiction newsletters and news magazines, such as *Locus, Thrust,* and *Science Fiction Chronicle.* Mystery writers should check the publications of Mystery Writers of America and the independent publication *Mystery Scene*; writers of romances should read *Romantic Times* and the publications of Romance Writers of America; and so on.

The magazine *Publishers Weekly* requires some detailed discussion. *PW* is the professional organ of book publishing, and each issue is loaded with news, interviews, book reviews, industry gossip, and ads from many publishers for their new releases. Although any issue of *PW* can help you learn which presses are publishing what sort of material, you should pay special attention to its four biggest issues each year: the Spring Announcements issue (published in January or February), the American Booksellers Convention issue (published in April or May), the Summer Announcements issue (also published in April or May), and the Fall Announcements issue (published in August or September). Each of these special issues publishes lists of new releases from hundreds of publishers, as well as advertisements from hundreds of presses announcing their new books. This is an indispensable basic resource for novelists and other book authors who wish (or need) to market their own books.

If you have a book for younger readers, the semiannual Children's Books issues of *PW* are virtually required reading. These are huge issues, published in spring and fall, usually in February and sometime during the summer. They are very similar to *PW*'s Spring and Fall Announcements issues, but they cover books for readers ages 17 and younger.

If you have a book that might be appropriate for a religious, spiritual, occult, or new age publisher, check *PW*'s semiannual Religious Books issues, published in March and September or October.

Not as helpful as *PW*, but still a useful resource, is the magazine *Library Journal*, which also publishes long lists of new and forthcoming titles, ads from many different publishers, and a wide range of book reviews. Particularly useful are its New Books for Spring and New Books for Fall issues, published in January or February and August or September, respectively. Writers of books for children should consult *LJ*'s sister publication, *School Library Journal*.

Using some of the resources listed above, make up a list of potential markets for your work. The next step is optional, but highly recommended. Pay a visit to a major library. Browse through the magazine collection and the fiction books, and make note of any magazines or book publishers that look like they publish the type of project you wish to sell.

Next, do the same thing at a major newsstand or bookstore. If you're researching magazine markets, find the newsstand or bookstore with the widest range of magazines that you can. If you're researching book markets, go to the largest bookstore in the area. It's a good idea to go to two or three different stores, since each will carry some publications that the others do not. If at all possible, try to go to a major city to do this browsing; the wealth of information you'll gather and the money, time, and aggravation you'll save later will make the trip more than worthwhile.

Special-interest bookstores are excellent places to do market research. Many bookstores, particularly those in larger cities, now specialize in one or two areas, such as religious (usually Christian) publications, gay or lesbian material, science fiction and fantasy, mystery, romance, new age/spiritual publications, material for children and young adults, and so on. Most of these bookstores carry magazines as well as books. If you've got genre material or material for a specialized audience to sell, check the Yellow Pages to see if there's a specialty bookshop in that genre or topic near you.

By now you should have a good-sized list of possible markets. You're ready to narrow down that list to those markets that are genuinely appropriate for your work.

If you have a book or book proposal to sell, your next step is to look at publishers' recent or current catalogs. This is the key to researching book markets. Most presses will send you their current catalogs on request at no charge; you may make your request by either mail or phone.

There are other, less reliable, sources of catalogs. Some libraries and bookstores keep the book catalogs they receive on file, and will let you look through them. There is also an annual microfiche publication called *Publishers Catalogs Annual* that includes recent catalogs from hundreds of publishers. Some libraries get *Publishers Catalogs Annual* each year.

Do be sure to get either current or very recent catalogs;

nothing else will give you an accurate picture of what publishers are publishing now.

Book packagers rarely or never issue catalogs, and they almost never advertise or receive coverage in *Publishers Weekly* and other magazines. For this reason, it is neither necessary nor very possible to do much market research into book packagers. Do, however, carefully read the section of *Literary Market Place* called Book Producers. You can also, if you wish, call each packager that interests you; ask for the names and publishers of some of its recent projects, and ask what kind of material it is currently seeking.

If you wish to market shorter material, your next step is to get your hands on some recent issues of every publication that you feel might be appropriate for one or more of your pieces. Ideally, you want the current issue and the one or two immediately previous ones.

The most inexpensive source for many of these publications will of course be libraries. Your best bets will be the main branches of big-city libraries and the libraries of major universities. Many libraries are now linked together via computer networks, so if a library doesn't have the magazine or newspaper you're looking for, ask the reference librarian to see if any other library in the area carries it. (Find out exactly which libraries are included in this data base and which ones are not. Some data bases, for example, may include all the public libraries in the area, but no college or university libraries.) If a magazine or newspaper is not available in any library in your area, you can order the most recent issue through inter-library loan.

Another option is to visit a large newsstand or bookstore and purchase copies of the magazines and newspapers that interest you. A good newsstand or bookstore will carry an astonishingly wide array of publications.

You can, of course, simply order the most recent issue of any publication directly from the publisher. A few publishers will send a recent sample copy to freelance writers on request at no charge; some will send a free copy if you provide a self-addressed envelope of sufficient size and adequate postage; others will demand that you pay the cover price; and still others will want the cover price plus a fee for postage and handling. You may make your request for a sample copy by either mail or phone (I prefer phoning). Explain that you're a freelance writer interested in sending that publication some of your work.

Once you've got the sample issues in front of you, go through them carefully. You don't have to read every item in every publication, but do pay attention to each publication's contents, slant, and intended audience. To what lengths do its fiction pieces run? Does it publish newer writers regularly, rarely, or never?

You can trust what you see in the publication itself. You *cannot* necessarily trust market notices in writers' magazines and directories, or writers' guidelines issued by the publication. If a market notice says that a magazine prints no genre fiction, but in the magazine you read a horror story, you can assume that it does seriously consider horror stories. If a market directory says a publication prints material of from 3,000-10,000 words, and you see a 1,000-word short-short story in that publication, feel free to send it some of your very short work. Believe the publication itself over any notice, listing, or set of printed guidelines.

There's one exception to this rule, however, and that's work by famous people. Most magazines and newspapers will break their own rules for the likes of Garrison Keillor, Grace Paley, Isaac Bashevis Singer, or Tama Janowitz. Those same publications will *not* break them for you. When you see a piece by a star or superstar, don't try to infer any generalities from it; base your judgment on the remainder of the publication.

EDITORS

Once you've carefully read through all the appropriate magazines, newspapers, or book publishers' catalogs, you'll have narrowed down your list of potential markets to those that are excellent places to submit your work. Now you're finally ready to determine which editors at those markets are the right ones to approach. How can you locate the best editors for your work depends on what type of market you are dealing with. I'll discuss the four market categories one at a time.

Magazines

Near the front of virtually every magazine, usually on (or within a few pages of) the contents page, is a list of staff people. This is called a *masthead*, and it will usually list most or all of the magazine's editors.

If the magazine is small or medium-sized (examples: *Isaac Asimov's Science Fiction Magazine, Shenandoah, The Gamut*), check the masthead for a Fiction Editor. If one is listed, send your manuscript to this person. If no Fiction Editor is listed, send your manuscript to the Editor or Editor-in-Chief. Virtually all local, regional, and genre magazines fall into this category, as do most literary magazines, most religious magazines, and most special-interest magazines that publish some fiction.

In the case of magazines with large circulations and/or international reputations, (examples: *Playboy, Redbook, The Atlantic, The Saturday Evening Post, The Paris Review*), you must be more careful. The editors-in-chief and fiction editors at these publication tend to read few or no unsolicited manuscripts from writers they do not know personally or by reputation. If you send your work to too highly placed an editor, he or she will probably pass it on, unread, to the person in charge of the slush pile. Obviously, you don't want this to happen.

Check the mastheads of these publications carefully. If an Assistant Fiction Editor or Associate Fiction Editor is listed, this is the proper person to approach with your work. If no separate editors are listed for fiction, submit your work to either an Assistant Editor or an Associate Editor. (If there is more than one of either, pick one using your intuition.) In the rare case that a Fiction Editor is listed but an Assistant or Associate Fiction Editor is not, you may approach the Fiction Editor.

If you are contemplating sending your work to *The New Yorker*, you will learn (if you have not learned already) that this magazine has no masthead. If you want your manuscript to receive a genuinely careful reading at *The New Yorker*, you first need to learn the name of one of its fiction editors from a literary agent, an editor, another writer, or someone else with knowledge of or connections with *The New Yorker*. (*The New Yorker*'s fiction editors are not listed in any market directory or other reference book; only its editor-in-chief is listed. Do *not* send your work to this person; if you do, it will end up in the slush pile.)

Very important: the names of magazine editors listed in market directories and market notices in writers' magazines are not always reliable. *Trust the masthead more than any other source of names.* Occasionally a magazine will deliberately list as its "editor" in a market notice the flunky who oversees the slush pile. Or a large magazine might list only its editor-in-chief, who does not read unsolicited manuscripts from writers he or she does not already know. If you send your work to this person, it will go straight into the slush pile.

If you wish to submit your work to foreign markets, you may have a hard time locating copies of all the publications that interest you. (You'll be surprised, however, at the number of foreign publications, particularly British ones, that a good newsstand, bookstore, or university or big-city library will carry.) And foreign publishers do not often send free copies of their publications to writers overseas (the cost of postage is prohibitive). Therefore, when investigating foreign markets, you may be forced to rely on writers' magazines, newsletters, and market directories.

Newspapers

As I explained in Chapter 1, the only significant markets for fiction in newspapers are magazine supplements. The procedure for locating the proper editors at these supplements is the same as for other magazines: get a copy of each one that interests you and look at the masthead, usually published on the inside front cover or contents page. If there is a Fiction Editor, send your work to that person; if there isn't, direct your manuscript to the supplement's Editor-in-Chief.

In the very rare cases where there is no masthead, simply

call up the newspaper and ask the operator, "Who's the editor of your Sunday magazine section?"

Book Publishers

Books, of course, have no masthead that lists editors. But there are two excellent resources that will provide much of the same information: the annual reference book, *Literary Market Place*, and the magazine *Publishers Weekly*. These are discussed below.

If you have a genre book or proposal to sell, writers' newsletters and news magazines that focus on that genre can be very helpful. These are often published by the organizations of professional writers in the particular genres (e.g., Mystery Writers of America), but some excellent newsletters and magazines are published independently. When a market notice in a genre newsletter or magazine provides an editor's name, use it; market information in these publications is usually very reliable.

If you have a mainstream project, or if you have a genre project and a publisher that interests you is not discussed in any genre newsletter, you'll have to do a little research. The place to begin is *Literary Market Place*.

LMP is published annually, around November, for the following year. It lists hundreds of U.S. and Canadian presses, and is a thorough, accurate, and very useful book. Because editors change jobs with astonishing frequency in book publishing, it is essential that you use only the current edition.

Begin using *LMP* by looking up each publisher that interests you in the index in back. This index will tell you exactly where to find information on each press. For example, if you wish to submit your fantasy novel to Del Rey Books, the index will tell you to look under Ballantine Books, of which Del Rey is a division.

Some publishing houses that publish both adult books and books for younger readers will have two separate listings, one for adult books and another for junior books, juveniles, or books for young readers. Be sure to refer to the appropriate listing.

Once you've turned to the correct listing for the publisher you're interested in, you'll find a list of between one and two hundred names and job titles. Scan this list carefully and completely, looking for the names of editors. The larger the publisher, the more names are likely to be listed, and the more careful you need to be about picking a name.

Let's start with the smallest presses—those that publish ten or fewer books per year. No more than one to four editors will probably be listed for each. If a separate fiction editor is listed, send your work to that person. If there is a separate editor for the type of project you wish to sell (e.g., a western, romance, children's book, young adult book, etc.), direct your submission to that editor.

In most cases, however, small houses won't have department editors. In such cases, simply send your work to the Editor or Editor-in-Chief. If no Editor or Editor-in-Chief is listed at all (as is the case with some very small houses), send your work to the person with the title of Publisher.

The purpose of sorting through editors' names in this fashion is to locate the person most likely to be interested in buying good books from among its unsolicited submissions. At firms with three or more editors, the editor-in-chief rarely reads many unsolicited manuscripts from writers he or she does not know personally or by reputation. Sending your work to this person could cause it to end up in the slush pile, while picking an editor in a slightly lower position may get you a serious and interested reading.

Now let's suppose you're investigating a large or medium-sized press. (In this discussion I'll call any press that does 11-25 books a year medium-sized, and one that publishes more than 25, large.) First, read its entire listing in *LMP* from beginning to end. If you have a book for younger readers, check to see if the house has a separate listing for a young readers, juvenile, or junior books division. If you have a genre book, see if the press has a separate editor, or more than one editor, for that genre. If no genre editor is listed, check for a fiction editor. If you have a mainstream adult book, also look for a fiction editor. If, in either case, no fiction editor is listed, make your selection from among the various editors, senior editors, associate editors, and other such titles. Don't pick the top editor unless no lesser editors are listed; go one step down, to a senior editor or editor.

If you have a book for young readers, be aware that there are almost never separate genre or fiction editors for these books. With few exceptions, the same editors consider both mainstream and genre material, and both fiction and nonfiction.

If a press has two or more editors in the areas you're looking for (romance, male adventure, young adult books, etc.) and they're given equal billing, pick one by playing your hunch. But if the editors have different titles—for example, Editor-in-Chief and Senior Editor—pick the editor one step below the top dog in that area.

Things get a little more complicated for a large or medium-sized press that you know from your research publishes an on-going line of genre or special-topic books (e.g., lesbian fiction, novels by new writers, etc.). If no editor for that line is listed, then *LMP* hasn't given you sufficient information. Check *Writer's Market, Novel and Short Story Writer's Market, Children's Writer's and Illustrator's Market*, and genre newsletters and magazines for this person's name. If none of these resources supplies this information, you'll need to call the publisher to ask for the name of this editor. One exception to this procedure: if the press publishes *only* books in that genre or on that topic, look for a fiction editor, senior editor, editor, etc. as explained above; this will be the proper person to approach with your work.

The great majority of book publishers that issue fiction titles are listed in *LMP*, but some smaller houses do not receive listings. If a press is not listed in *LMP*, check the following reference books: *International Directory of Little Magazines and Small Presses, Novel and Short Story Writer's Market, Writer's Market*, and/or *Children's Writer's and Illustrator's Market*. As with *LMP*, it's important to use current editions.

If you want to locate the names of editors and publishers outside of the U.S. and Canada, you'll need to use one or more of these books: *Directory of Publishing, International Literary Market Place, International Writers and Artists Yearbook*, and the *International Directory of Little Magazines and Small Presses*.

A more direct approach to locating editors is to call up each publisher and ask for the appropriate editor's name. At a small or medium-sized publishing house, you can simply call up and ask whoever answers, "What's the name of your editor?" or, if you prefer, "What's the name of your acquisitions editor?" (This is an editor who "acquires" manuscripts — that is, reads and buys them for publication.)

Your strategy will need to be slightly different at large presses. Your call will probably be answered by a switchboard operator or receptionist, who will know very little. Ask for the editorial department; the person who answers there will probably be a secretary. Ask this person, "Can you tell me who's editing your _____ books now?" Fill in the blank with the appropriate genre, readership (e.g., young adults), or line (e.g., gay novels) — or, if none of these apply, with the word "fiction."

In most cases, these direct inquiries will get you the appropriate names. You may be asked, "Why do you want to know?" Answer honestly: "I'm a writer with a book project that I think is appropriate for your house, and I'd like to know the name of the proper person to send it to."

The great majority of small and medium-sized book publishers are willing to give out the names of their editors. Some of the larger ones, however, are not. Your request may sometimes be denied, or you might be told to send your work to simply The Editor or Editorial Department. A little diplomacy will sometimes work here. For example, you might say, "I hate to send something to someone without being able to address it by name. It's like getting a piece of junk mail marked 'Occupant.' Can you please give me a name to write to?"

You can also use phone inquiries in a working-backward process to locate book editors. Make a list of some contemporary fiction writers you admire, and/or recent fiction books you've enjoyed. If your own project is a genre book, list books and writers in the same genre; if your project is for children, middle readers, or young adults, pick writers and books appropriate for the same age group. Omit from this list bestselling books and writers.

Next, go get some of the titles on your list at a library or bookstore. If you've listed writers by name instead of by their works, any of their recent books will do. Use *Books in Print, Paper-*

bound Books in Print, Forthcoming Books, Canadian Books in Print, and *Small Press Record of Books in Print* to obtain a list of titles by any author.

Your task is now to locate the original U.S. publisher of each book. Check the copyright page; the original U.S. publisher should be noted here. If no previous publisher is listed, then the publisher of the edition you are looking at is almost certainly the original U.S. publisher.

Writers living in Canada should modify this strategy slightly; so should American writers who have come across a book published in a Canadian edition. See if the copyright page lists an American press that has previously published the book or is publishing it simultaneously with the Canadian publisher. If such an American press is listed, note its name; this is the firm you'll need to call. If more than one American publishing house is listed, note the one that published the earlier edition of the book. If no American press is listed at all, check to see if another Canadian firm has issued an earlier edition of the book. If no other publishing house in any country is listed, the publisher of the edition you're looking at is very likely the work's original publisher.

If a previous Canadian press is listed, you'll have to get your hands on a copy of an edition published by that Canadian house. Check the copyright page of *that* edition for a simultaneous or previous American publisher; if none is listed, the publisher of the edition you are looking at is the press you should call.

Once you've determined the original North American publisher of a book, get its phone number from directory assistance or one of the reference books listed on pages 29-30. Then call up that publisher using the guidelines on pages 39-40. Ask, "Can you tell me the name of the editor who acquired _____ (title of book) by _____ (author)?" If the publisher has issued several books by the same writer, simply ask, "Can you tell me the name of _____'s editor?" This is the person to whom you should send your work. However, don't hang up once you have a name. Be sure to ask, "Is he/she still an editor with your firm? " If the answer is no, ask where that editor is working now; about half the time, the person you're speaking with will know. If he or she *doesn't* know, check the index of *Literary Market Place* for the editor's name. If it's listed, the index will tell you where and in what capacity he or she works now.

Note that if a writer you admire has published books with several different presses, you can use this strategy to come up with the names of several different editors.

Book Packagers

Fiction writers' dealings with book packagers are limited to three situations: 1) when a packager needs material for a fiction series it is overseeing or developing; 2) when a writer wishes to propose a series of his or her own to the packager; and 3) when a writer has an unusual illustrated project to sell.

In the first circumstance, the name of the series editor will normally be listed in any market notice. (This information will almost always be reliable.) If no editor's name is listed, or if you don't find a market notice, the proper thing to do is call the packager's office and ask, "Can you tell me who's editing your _____ series?" Nine out of ten times you'll be given the editor's name.

If you wish to propose a fiction series of your own, or if you have an illustrated project to offer, you can find the names you need in *Literary Market Place*, under the heading Book Producers, a term synonymous with book packagers. Book packagers typically have one to four editors and produce four to twelve books a year, so treat these listings as you would listings for small publishers. If only one editor (perhaps called the director, creative director, or president) is listed, send your work to that person. If a packager has exactly two editors, approach the higher-level person; if both people have equal status, pick either one. If a firm has three or more editors, don't contact the most senior editor or the director; pick someone one step lower.

Another Important Option

There is one other way to locate appropriate editors for your work: seek recommendations from your personal and professional contacts (your agent, other writers, other editors, etc.). The right people can not only recommend editors to you, but can recommend you and your work to editors. For a complete discussion of this subject, see Chapter 8.

Some Notes on Names

Whenever you get an editor's or agent's name, double-check its spelling. You are not going to make a very good impression if your manuscript or letter arrives with the name misspelled on the envelope. Also, when possible, make note of whether an editor or agent is male or female. People named Chris, Marion, Lynn, and so forth might be of either sex. Over the phone or in person, simply ask, "Is it Mr. or Ms.?," and ask for the name to be spelled out. In *Literary Market Place* and a few other reference volumes you can double-check spellings of names in the index; reference books won't usually indicate someone's sex, however.

CHECKLISTS

Ways to locate appropriate agents:
- Ask your personal and professional contacts (editors, other writers, etc.).
- List some contemporary writers whose work you admire. Using reference books and the telephone, learn the names and addresses of their agents.
- Read the Rights, Talk of the Trade, People, and New Ventures columns in *Publishers Weekly*.
- Carefully read the agents' listings in reference books: *Literary Agents of North America*, *Literary Market Place*, *Novel and Short Story Writer's Market*, *Writer's Market*, and *Children's Writer's and Illustrator's Market*. For foreign agents, check the reference books listed on pages 26-27.

Ways to locate appropriate editors:
- First, do some initial market research to determine which publishers or publications are appropriate for your work. Use the reference books, magazines, and newsletters listed on pages 28-30.

- Continue your market research by visiting a major library, bookstore, or newsstand. Look at the current issue of each publication that interests you. If you have a book or book proposal to sell, look carefully at publishers' current catalogs.
- Locate magazine editors (including the editors of magazine supplements in newspapers) by looking at mastheads in current issues.
- Locate book editors by using the current issue of *Literary Market Place*.
- Locate editors at book packagers by looking under Book Producers in *Literary Market Place*.
- Use the guidelines in this chapter to choose the proper editor from among those listed on mastheads and in reference books. Avoid picking anyone too high or too low.
- When necessary or appropriate, call publishers directly to ask for editors' names.
- Ask your personal and professional contacts for recommendations and referrals.

CHAPTER 4

MATTERS OF ETIQUETTE AND FORM

EVERY PROFESSION HAS ITS OWN standards and rules of etiquette. Freelance writing is no exception. Many of these rules and standards are somewhat arbitrary; nevertheless, because they are widely used and widely accepted, the more you pay attention to and follow them, the more you will be perceived as a working professional, and the more likely you are to have your work read seriously and carefully. Indeed, doing things properly and professionally can sometimes make the difference between selling your work and having it rejected.

This chapter will go through these standards in detail. If you'd like an exhaustive discussion of the subject, read William Brohaugh's excellent book, *Professional Etiquette for Writers* (Writer's Digest Books).

MANUSCRIPT FORM

What follows are basic guidelines for prose manuscripts: short stories, novellas, novels, book proposals, and other fiction (and nonfiction) of any length. Manuscript formats for other types of writing are quite different from those discussed here. *The Writer's Digest Guide to Manuscript Formats* by Dian Dincin Buchman and Seli Groves (Writer's Digest Books) provides detailed information on the proper form for manuscripts of all types.

Samples of proper manuscript form appear on the following pages:

- First page of a short prose manuscript: page 47
- Cover page for a book or book proposal: page 48
- First page of text in a book or book proposal: page 49
- Later page of a prose manuscript of any length: page 50

Your manuscript should be typed on plain 8½-by-11-inch paper, thick enough that you cannot easily see through it. Onionskin is not acceptable, nor is any color other than white. Your best value is standard photocopying (xerox) or spirit duplicating (ditto) paper, which runs $3-6 per ream (500 sheets) at office supply stores. Ask for twenty-pound bond; this is the standard weight for manuscript paper. Avoid erasable paper, which smears easily and is expensive. Do not use paper with holes, lines, or rounded edges.

Double-space your entire manuscript, with these two exceptions: 1) epigraphs, and quotations from songs, movies, other literary works, etc. that are two lines or longer should be single spaced, with margins an inch wider than the rest of your text; 2) names, addresses, and phone numbers typed on your first page (or, in the case of books and book proposals, on your cover page) should be single spaced.

Always type your work neatly, on one side of the page only, using a standard typeface—that is, one that is clear, readable, and in regular use. Avoid unusual typefaces such as Script, Orator, Grande, Italic, Quadro, Cubic, or Gothic. Each letter should be clear and dark; this means keeping your typewriter keys clean and using a good, dark ribbon. Only black ink is acceptable. Any typewriter in good repair, including the cheapest manual, will produce clear, readable text.

Manuscripts may be typed on a *letter-quality* computer printer or typewriter; "near-letter-quality" is not good enough. Editors read tens of thousands of words a day, and their eyes are often tired; the easier your manuscript is to read, the more likely an editor is to think favorably of it. If you don't have a letter-quality printer, rent or borrow one. Any kind of letter-quality printer will do, from dot matrix to laser jet. A good rule of thumb: if you can see individual dots making up letters, the typeface is not letter-quality.

Scott Edelstein
2706 West 43 Street, Suite 102
Minneapolis, MN 55410
(612) 929-9123

About 4500 words

COMFORT

by Scott Edelstein

Ever since I was a little boy, my mother suffered from chronic headaches. She'd usually get them in late afternoon, especially when the days were hot and muggy. She hated to take pills, and when one of her headaches would set in, she'd lie down on her bed, close her eyes, and have my father sit beside her and rub her forehead. Almost always, the headaches would go away after a few minutes of rubbing. This impressed me immensely, and probably had something to do with my becoming a massage therapist fifteen years later. From the start, however, my mother had wanted me to be a doctor.

One hot, thick summer afternoon when I was six, my mother called me up to her bedroom. My father was away in Columbus on business, and she said to me, "Bobby, would you like to try rubbing my head for me?"

"Sure," I said, delighted at the chance to do a grownup's job.

Scott Edelstein
2706 West 43 Street, Suite 102
Minneapolis, MN 55410
(612) 929-9123

Agent:
Bobbe Siegel
41 West 83 Street
New York, NY 10024
(212) 877-4985

IT ALL HAPPENED SO FAST

A Novel by Scott Edelstein

Proposed Length: 75,000 words

Chapter One

When Marjorie saw Dan for the first time in eleven years, her first thought was, "I should have become a doctor."

Dan obviously needed healing. His right arm--the arm that was always falling asleep when they would lie side by side, his arms curled around her--was in a cast, and his walk was awkward and tense, as if he were avoiding small obstacles. The smile he gave her was sincere but somehow laden with effort.

She took his valise and led him down the crowded concourse, wondering if he looked as abused and vulnerable to strangers as he did to her. Then she wondered why the opinions of strangers seemed to be important to her.

"How was the flight?" she heard herself ask.

"Wet and dirty," he said, giving her another tense smile. "We hit an air pocket just as the steward was handing me my supper.

Comfort/2

"Sit next to me," she said, "and put your fingers on my temples." Her eyes were closed and she looked very pale. I put my dirty hands on her forehead, but I didn't know where the temples were. She reached up and repositioned my hands, then showed me how to rub. "See?" she said. "In circles. Press down, but not too hard. It's a bad one, so rub carefully." Then she put her hand back down at her side.

I started rubbing as best I could. She kept her eyes closed and her mouth was open just a little.

I worked on her forehead until I was tired and bored. Then I said, "Is it any better, Mom?"

She smiled slightly and lifted my hands off her forehead. "A little." She sat up, the squeezed her eyes shut tightly and lay back down again. "Are you okay?" I asked. She didn't answer.

I started rubbing again, but after a few seconds she sat back up, much more slowly, and propped herself up on her arms. "I'm going to get some water," she said in a whisper. She stood up very carefully, wobbled for a second, and then walked slowly out of the bedroom, holding her right arm half outstretched in front of her.

I lay down on the bed and wiggled my legs impatiently, singing a TV commercial to myself. Then I heard my mother groan, and there was a horrible plop as she collapsed in the hallway.

I ran out into the hall and saw her lying unconscious, her body limp and twisted up.

Two type sizes are acceptable for manuscripts: pica (10 pitch) and the slightly smaller elite (12 pitch). Do not use anything larger or smaller.

Your margins should be large enough so that editors can write typesetting and design instructions in them. I recommend one-inch margins on all four sides.

With the exception of the first page of your manuscript—and, in the case of books and proposals, your cover page as well—each page should have a heading at the top. This should include the page number and one or more words that clearly identify the piece. This will usually be the title; if the title is long, use one or two key words from it. If you like, you may also type your last name as part of your heading; separate it from your title with a slash.

Type your heading about an inch from the top of the paper, at either the left or right margin. Your text should begin three or four lines below the heading.

Your first page of text will follow a different format from later pages. In the case of books and book proposals, the top half of your first page will be completely blank; the bottom half will contain double-spaced text. In the exact center of the page, four to six lines above the beginning of your text, type "Chapter One." If your chapters have titles, drop down two lines and, centered, type the chapter title. Your text should begin four lines below this.

The rules for the first page of manuscripts other than books and proposals are a bit different. Once again your text will begin halfway down the page. The top half of the page, however, will contain useful information for editors, agents, and other publishing professionals. In the upper left of the page, about an inch from the top, type your name, flush against the left-hand margin. If you are using a pseudonym for the piece, your *real* name still goes here. Drop down *one* line, not two, and type your street address or post office box. One line below this type your city, state or province, and zip or postal code; add your country on this line as well if you live outside of the U.S. and Canada, or if you plan to submit the manuscript to a publication outside of the two countries. Drop down one more line and type your phone number(s). If you have both work and home numbers, list both, and indicate which is which, so that editors can easily reach you by phone.

If you are a member of a professional writers' organization and wish to indicate that membership, drop down two lines below your phone number(s) and type, "Member, Western Writers of America" (or whatever) against the left margin. If you have no such membership or do not wish to list any affiliation, leave this spot blank. If you wish to list two or three such memberships, list each on a separate line, single-spaced. (See pages 91-92 for a detailed discussion on listing appropriate memberships.)

In the upper right of the page, type the approximate length of the piece — e.g., "3,500 words" or "About 5,000 words." Round to the nearest 100 words if the piece is 1,500 words or less; to the nearest 500 words if the manuscript is 1,500-10,000 words; to the nearest 1,000 words if the piece is 10,000-25,000 words; and to the nearest 5,000 words for longer works.

Drop down about twenty lines. Type the title of your piece, centered from left to right, in all capital letters. Two lines below this, also centered, type your by-line, e.g., "by Bill Shakespeare." If you wish the piece to be published under a pseudonym, use it here. The first sentence of your piece should begin 4-6 lines below your by-line.

If your manuscript has two or more co-authors, your first page should be designed slightly differently. One option is to provide information on both (or all) authors in the upper left, in this manner:

Scott Edelstein
2706 West 43 Street, Suite 102
Minneapolis, MN 55410
(612) 929-9123

Harriet Beecher Stowe
8131 LaSalle Avenue
Richfield, MN 55416
(612) 555-3490

If you choose this option, drop down only one line instead of two between a writer's phone number(s) and his or her professional affiliation(s).

If you prefer, you may provide the address and phone number(s) of only one of the authors, who will serve as the representative of all the collaborators. Do, however, list the names of all the co-authors above the address, in this way:

Scott Edelstein
Harriet Beecher Stowe
2706 West 43 Street, Suite 102
Minneapolis, MN 55410
(612) 929-9123

If you have a book or proposal, you will need a cover page. This will be the first page your reader sees. It will contain the same information as the first page of a shorter manuscript, but it will contain no text.

On your cover page, type your name, address, phone number(s), organizational affiliation(s), title, and by-line just as you would on page one of a short piece. If you like, you may add "A Novel By," "A Novella By," or "A Story By" before your by-line. Your word-count, however, belongs not in the upper right, but about fifteen lines below your by-line, centered from left to right. If the manuscript is a proposal, you should type "Proposed Length: 70,000 words" or "Projected Length: 70,000 words" instead of simply "About 70,000 words."

If the book or proposal is being represented by an agent (but *not* if you are sending it to an agent to see if he or she will represent it), you should also indicate the agent's name, address, and phone number. You may do this in either the upper or lower right of your cover page, single spaced, in the same manner in which you listed information about yourself.

If you have an agent and wish to keep your own address and phone number(s) completely private, you may omit them from the upper left. Directly under your name, type "c/o" and the name of your agent. Then list your *agent's* address and phone number instead of your own, and leave both the upper and lower right of the page blank. If you wish to keep your identity private as well, type your pseudonym in the upper left instead of your name, as well as in your by-line.

The page immediately following your cover page will usually be your author biography. This may be followed by other items (endorsements, a table of contents, etc.), or it may be followed immediately by your first page of text. Use common sense in numbering pages. Your author biography will usually be page one, and your actual text may not begin until page five or six; this is fine. All "frontmatter," such as your table of contents and author biography, should normally be double-spaced.

At the end of any manuscript, whatever its length, simply stop typing. It is neither necessary nor appropriate to type "End," "The End," or "30."

Making Corrections

Your manuscript should be neat, clean, easy to read, and free of major corrections. Like it or not, a professional-looking manuscript is slightly more likely to get published than one that's just as well written but sloppy-looking.

Small corrections, such as changing, deleting, or adding a word, may be made in black pen (black photocopies best). If you need to make a major correction, or more than four or five small corrections on the same page, you'll need to retype part or all of the page. If you have a word processor, you should run a new, corrected page to fix all but the smallest errors. If you have only a typewriter, there are two ways to make good-sized changes without having to retype the whole page. One is to use correction tape: thin strips of sticky white tape, available at office supply stores. Place a strip of tape over a line of text, type the change on the tape, and photocopy the page. Another option is to change your original copy by typing the corrected text on a separate page, cutting it out, and carefully taping it over the old text. If you align the text well, none of the cutting or taping will show on a photocopy.

You should of course also edit and proofread every manuscript carefully, so that it is free of errors of spelling, punctuation, grammar, and diction.

Other Tips on Manuscript Form

• *Novellas* How you intend to market your novella will affect its format. If you wish to sell it as a small book, prepare a cover page and first page as you would for a novel; if you wish to market the piece to magazines and/or anthologies, omit the cover page and prepare a first page as you would for a short story. If you plan to market your novella both ways, you'll need to prepare both a cover page and two different first pages.

• *Submission on Computer Disks* Although some editors now accept submissions on computer disks, never submit a work of fiction on a disk unless you *know* that an editor accepts *and prefers* to read material in this form. In those very rare cases when you do make a disk submission, be sure to attach a hard-copy cover letter.

• *Submitting Photocopies* To guard against loss or damage, hang onto your original copy of each manuscript and submit a clear, dark, high-quality photocopy. If something does happen to a photocopy, it is a simple matter to make another copy from your original. No editor will object to seeing a photocopied manuscript.

• *Word-Counts* To get an accurate estimate of the length of any manuscript, count the number of words on one full page. Multiply this number by the number of pages; then make allowances for pages which are partly blank. If you are using a computer or word processor, you may use the alternate method of dividing the total number of characters by 5.5.

• *Variations* In other books for writers you may see some small variations on the manuscript formats described in this chapter. Most of these variations are legitimate and acceptable. However, the precise formats described here are the ones most commonly used.

• *Copyright and Rights Available* If your piece has not been previously published, do *not* include a copyright notice on your manuscript; such a notice is neither necessary nor appropriate, since under U.S. law a piece is automatically copyrighted and protected as soon as it is created. If *and only if* a piece has been previously published, or is scheduled to be published, in whole or part, you should type a copyright notice two spaces below your word-count. This should state where and when the piece was originally published (or will be published). For instance: "Originally published in *Druid Romance*, May 1990. Copyright 1990 by Nymph Publications."

Never indicate on any manuscript what rights you wish to sell. This will need to be negotiated between you and your publisher. Different publishers may want to buy different sets of rights.

Quite a few books on writing contradict the advice in the above two paragraphs. Some suggest that you indicate on your manuscript what rights you wish to sell. Others urge writers to type copyright notices on unpublished manuscripts. Not only are both these things unnecessary and illogical, but they'll make you look like an amateur, and could predispose editors to decide against your manuscript. Some otherwise excellent books offer incorrect guidance on these two topics.

• *Social Security Number* Don't put your social security number on your manuscript or in your cover letter. This is unnecessary and looks amateurish to editors. If and when a publisher needs this information, you'll be asked for it.

• *Clipping and Packaging* If your manuscript is eighty pages or less, it should be held together with a paper clip of appropriate size. Large paper clips (meant to hold 25 pages or more) are called butterfly clamps, and are available at office supply stores. Never staple a manuscript intended for publication.

Full-length books should be placed, unclipped, inside two-part manuscript boxes. These have a separate base and lid, and are large enough to hold a ream (500 sheets) of paper. These are sometimes hard to find, but they are usually available through printers and some of the larger office supply stores. Be sure to get plain grey or white boxes; don't use boxes with company names or logos on them. Type two labels, one with the book's title and your by-line, the other with your name, address, and phone number(s); put the first in the exact center of the box lid, where it will be easily visible; place the name and address label four to five inches directly above or below it.

If you have a short book for children, a chapbook manuscript, or some other book of less than eighty pages, don't put it in a box. Instead, purchase a sturdy paper two-pocket folder, the type without a gusset (a strip used for binding in three-hole paper). This should be grey, black, brown, or dark blue. Clip the manuscript together and place it in the right-hand pocket. Type two labels, one with your title and by-line, another with your name, address, and phone number(s); affix them to the front of your folder just as you would to the box lid for a full-length book.

If you have a book proposal, prepare a folder just as you would for a short book in the paragraph above. For detailed instructions on assembling a book proposal, see Chapter 12.

● *Series* If you have *extensive* publishing credits, including at least one or two fiction books sold to major publishers, you may propose a series to a book publisher or packager. A series proposal should consist of an overview or outline of the entire series, plus either *one* complete book for the series or a proposal for such a book. Your series outline/overview should be double-spaced and 3-8 pages; the other aspects of the format are up to you.

● *Illustrations* If you have illustrations that accompany a manuscript, keep the originals; submit slides or photocopies. Illustrations on paper should be integrated into the text, though illustrations need not receive page numbers. Slides should be placed in plastic sheets (usually holding twenty slides each), which go at the end of your manuscript. In the case of proposals, children's books, or other short books, place these sheets in the left-hand pocket of your folder.

● *Final Check* Before mailing any manuscript, look through it carefully to make sure every page is clean, neat, readable, complete, right-side-up, and in the proper order. You don't want to have your first-rate manuscript rejected because page 6 was missing, or because the bottom half of page 9 came out of the photocopier unreadably blurry.

MAILING YOUR WORK

In general, everything you mail should look neat, professional, and attractive. Manuscripts should usually be sent flat in previously unused 9-by-12-inch or 10-by-13-inch envelopes, either manila or white. Clasp envelopes are sturdier. Very short manuscripts (those four pages or shorter) may be sent, folded in thirds, in #10 (long) business envelopes. Anything too large for a 10-by-13 envelope should be sent in a padded mailing bag (sometimes called a jiffy bag), available in office supply stores. Be sure all packages are firmly sealed; use several staples or strong tape on mailing bags. Affix neatly typed mailing labels to all envelopes and packages; don't write on them in pen.

Each submission should include your manuscript(s), a cover letter, a self-addressed envelope (sometimes called an SAE), and return postage. (The term SASE, or self-addressed stamped envelope, refers to the combination of this envelope and postage.) If your work has been solicited—that is, if an editor or book packager has specifically asked to see it—you may omit the envelope and return postage. If an *agent* has asked to see it, however, do enclose an envelope and postage unless you are already one of his or her clients.

If you're submitting a short manuscript, paper-clip your cover letter on top of the first page, as if it were "page zero." If your manuscript is in a box, place the cover letter on top of the cover page; no clip is necessary. If your manuscript is in a two-pocket folder, you have several choices. You may simply clip the cover letter in front of your cover page; you may clip it, flat and face up, to the outside front cover of the folder, so that it is immediately visible; or you may fold it in thirds and place it in a #10 envelope on which you have typed the recipient's name. This envelope may be clipped to the outside front cover, or it may be placed in either inside pocket, on top of all pages and sticking halfway out, so that it is clearly visible.

Your return envelope or mailing bag should be new, and should be large enough for your manuscript to slip easily inside. Type and affix mailing labels carefully. The envelope or bag may be folded in half if necessary.

If you have a short manuscript, slip the envelope under the paper clip just behind the last page. If you've used a two-pocket folder, place the envelope behind the manuscript in the right-hand pocket. If your manuscript is in a box, fold the envelope and place it inside, under the last manuscript page. Manuscript bags are too bulky to be put inside folders and boxes, and thus should simply be placed, loose, inside your package.

Cardboard backing is neither necessary nor useful, and it inflates postage costs.

You should normally send your work first class or priority mail. Avoid fourth-class mail; it's not very much cheaper, can take a very long time, and looks less than professional. Do not send manuscripts via certified or registered mail, and do not insure your package. You may use UPS or another private courier service if you like; this won't impress anyone, though. Sending manuscripts via overnight delivery won't impress anyone either, though it will probably at least get their attention for a moment. Do not fax unsolicited manuscripts.

Be sure to include sufficient postage for your manuscript's return via first class or priority mail. Affix a mailing label on which you have typed "FIRST CLASS" to your return envelope or mailing bag.

If you are sending your work to any other country, you must enclose International Reply Coupons instead of return postage. IRCs are available at most post offices. Enclose the number of IRCs roughly equal to your cost in mailing the manuscript out of the country. (One exception: if you live in the U.S. and are submitting a manuscript to a Canadian publisher, add an extra IRC if your package weighs 13-16 ounces, and an additional IRC for each pound thereafter.) Affix a label on which you have typed "AIR MAIL" to your return envelope.

If you are submitting a short manuscript, slip your return postage or IRCs under the paper clip, on top of your cover letter. If your manuscript is in a box or folder, place your return postage in a #10 business envelope on which you have typed "Return Postage." Seal the envelope. If your manuscript is boxed, place the envelope on top of your cover letter. If your manuscript is in a folder, place the envelope in the left pocket of the folder, on top of all pages, so that it visibly sticks out.

There is an alternative to providing full return postage or multiple International Reply Coupons. You may, if you wish, enclose only a single stamp for one ounce of first class postage, or a single IRC; instead of a return envelope or mailing bag, enclose a regular #10 business envelope. Clip the stamp or IRC directly to the envelope. Include in your cover letter a paragraph such as this:

> I've enclosed a stamped business envelope [or a business envelope and one International Reply Coupon] for your reply. If my piece doesn't interest you, simply let me know via letter. There is no need to return the manuscript; I have additional copies.

Since photocopying a new manuscript is sometimes cheaper than the cost of return postage, this option may save you money.

Exceptions to the above guidelines for mailing manuscripts:

• When sending a manuscript out of the country, do not use first class or priority mail; use airmail. A special airmail rate is available for manuscripts sent to certain countries; check with the post office for details. Never send manuscripts surface mail; they can take months to arrive. Airmail usually takes ten days or less.

• Under certain circumstances it is an excellent idea to purchase the legal protection of a return receipt. This requires that you use certified mail. The receipt should show to whom your letter or package was delivered and the date on which it was delivered. Here are the three most common situations in which buying a return receipt is a wise move: when you have contracted to write a book based on a proposal and are mailing the final draft of the book to your editor; when you are mailing an agent a letter terminating your author-agent relationship; or when you have some reason to believe that your publisher is not to be trusted.

A small percentage of publishers — perhaps one out of twenty — will automatically acknowledge receipt of your manuscript with a postcard. Some writers request such notification routinely, and include with each submission a self-addressed, stamped postcard of their own, on which they have typed something like this: "Halfway House has received your manuscript, *The Old Man and the Cuisinart*." If you do this yourself, add a sentence to your cover letter asking the editor to drop the card in the mail to let you know that your manuscript has arrived safely; slip the card on top of the cover letter, where it will be clearly visible.

I don't include such a postcard with submissions myself, for two reasons: first, I've almost never had a manuscript lost or significantly delayed in the mail, even during the weeks before Christmas; second, a surprisingly large number of editors (perhaps 20 percent) neglect to mail notification postcards, even when authors have provided them.

WAITING

Once you've sent a manuscript to an editor, book packager, or agent, don't waste a minute waiting anxiously for a reply. Note down whom you sent it to and when you sent it; then forget about it, and get on with your next writing project. Once a month, review your list of what has been sent where.

If someone has not responded after three months, write or call to check on your manuscript. Be brief, to the point, and polite. Be sure to give the title of the piece and the date it was sent.

I usually prefer to call, because a phone call can be handled quickly and immediately. A letter, on the other hand, requires another letter in response, and someone too busy to respond promptly to a submission may well be too busy to respond to a letter of inquiry. If you do make a written inquiry, enclose a self-addressed, stamped #10 envelope for a reply.

One option you have is to enclose a checklist of possible responses—e.g., "Still under consideration," "Returned previously," "Never arrived," "Whereabouts unknown," etc. It's then a simple matter for the recipient to check one of these items and return the page or postcard to you.

If the response to your inquiry is, "I need a little more time," your reply should be, "Certainly, but I'd appreciate your getting to it within the next two weeks."

I've learned through experience that once someone has held on to a manuscript for four months without responding to it, he or she probably never will respond. Simply write off that submission. It is a waste of time to apply more pressure to this person, and there is no need to formally withdraw the manuscript. Just forget about it, and send it off to someone else.

There's one exception to this advice, however. If, during your four-month wait, the person to whom you sent your manuscript lets you know that he or she is quite interested in it but needs more time to make a decision, it makes sense to hang on a little longer. After four months have passed, make a polite phone call. Thereafter, sit tight. If you've received no word after six months, you may assume that, despite the initial interest, your piece has been lost, ignored, or forgotten.

In practice, the two most likely groups of people to take more than four months to respond to a manuscript are 1) book editors, and 2) editors at literary magazines and presses, particularly the smaller ones.

BUSINESS LETTERS

All correspondence involving your writing should be neatly and carefully typed in a standard business-letter format (block, semi-block, etc.). Single-space your text; double-space between paragraphs. See the letters on pages 71, 123, 125, and 128-129 for samples of proper business letter form. Correspondence not accompanying a manuscript should be sent in a long (#10) business envelope.

Normally you should use the same paper, typeface, type size, and letter-quality typewriter or printer for letters that you use for manuscripts. However, if you have good-looking personal stationery, or business stationery that identifies you as a writer, you may use this instead. Don't use stationery that is clearly inappropriate; for example, don't use your University of North Carolina stationery to write a cover letter for a submission to *Cavalier*.

Fiction writers do *not* need letterhead stationery, although for most nonfiction writers it is a very worthwhile investment. If you do purchase letterhead stationery, make sure it is understated and uncluttered. Avoid logos, designs, illustrations, or silly phrases. Your letterhead should include nothing more than your name, address, and phone number(s)—and, if you wish, either "Writer" or "Literary Services." I prefer the latter, which has yielded excellent results for me.

You should of course be concise and businesslike, though cordial, in all business letters.

NAMES AND TITLES

It is important to write to people in publishing by name, not merely by title. Write to "Gary Cobbs" or "Gary Cobbs, Mystery Editor," not merely to "Mystery Editor."

What about the titles of Mr., Ms., and Mrs.? When do you use them? Or do you simply address publishing people by their first names? Here are some useful guidelines:

Once you've established a relationship with an editor, agent, or other pubishing employee, you should feel free to use his or her first name or nickname. He or she will of course expect to use your first name or nickname as well. Publishing is a pretty informal industry. As a general rule, you may call someone whatever name he or she uses when signing letters or referring to himself or herself. If someone signs her letters "Sue," call her Sue; but if she signs them "Susan," call her Susan. Don't shorten

"Robert" to "Bob" unless you've seen or heard Bob do it himself. When in doubt, use the full first name.

When writing to someone you don't know, or with whom you have not yet established a personal or professional relationship, your best bet is to begin your letters, "Dear Harry Nelson," "Dear H.J. Klein," etc. This is more formal—and thus more appropriate—than using only a first name.

Avoid using Ms., Mrs., and Mr. entirely; it's too easy to annoy someone by incorrectly guessing their sex, or by using Ms. when she prefers Mrs. (or vice versa). Judging people's sex from their first name alone is a risky proposition at best.

USING THE PHONE

Never be afraid to call someone in publishing. When a phone call is faster, more efficient, or more convenient, use it without hesitation. But unnecessary phone calls can be annoying. When a letter will do just as well, write one.

Your phone manner should be businesslike but friendly, your conversation cordial but to the point. Publishing people (including agents) are sometimes hard to get hold of; don't be surprised if you often have to leave a message. For everyone's benefit, leave your reason for calling as well as your name and number(s). It's also an excellent idea to mention which times are best for reaching you. If your call is not returned within two business days, call again. If your second call is neither taken nor returned within two business days, write a letter.

Normally you shouldn't call anyone in publishing collect. However, if someone at a publishing company has specifically asked you to call, then you may call collect. Never call an agent collect for any reason.

CHECKLIST

Major points of etiquette and form:
- Use a letter-quality typewriter or printer for all manuscripts and letters.

- All manuscripts should be double-spaced.
- Make clear, dark photocopies of all manuscripts. Keep your original and submit the photocopies.
- Each page of every manuscript should be neat, attractive, and free of major corrections.
- Prepare a cover page for all books and book proposals.
- Carefully edit and proofread anything you've written before sending it out.
- Enclose a cover letter, a self-addressed envelope, and return postage with each unsolicited submission.
- Follow standard business letter form for all correspondence.
- Use the telephone whenever it will be faster, more efficient, or more convenient than writing a letter. But when a letter will do just as well, write rather than call.
- If an editor, book packager, agent, or other publishing professional has not responded to a submission within three months, follow up with a polite phone call or letter.

CHAPTER 5

APPROACHING EDITORS

ONCE YOU'VE DETERMINED THROUGH MARKET RESEARCH which editors to approach with your work, you want to be sure that you make contact in an acceptable, professional manner.

Traditionally, fiction writers have presented their work to editors in three ways: through query letters, through personal and professional contacts, and through unsolicited submissions. As you will see in a moment, with few exceptions, only the last two of these are worthwhile.

The most important rule in dealing with editors is to *always* contact them by name, not merely by title. This is the one tried-and-true way to get an editor's attention.

If a market notice in a writers' magazine or market directory says, "Send manuscripts to Fiction Editor" or "Address submissions to Editorial Department," *don't* follow this suggestion. Instead, find out the name of an appropriate editor using the strategies in Chapter 3. If you do not approach this editor by name, your work may go directly into the slush pile.

AVOIDING QUERIES

A *query letter*, also called simply a *query*, is a letter that briefly describes a piece of writing and asks the recipient if he or she would be willing to read it. After a moment's reflection, you'll realize that query letters are necessary only in cases where someone won't read unsolicited material. After all, if the editor of *The*

Imaginary Review will read unsolicited submissions, there's no point in asking her if she'll read yours; the answer is yes even before you send the query.

But what about people who don't read unsolicited material? Let's look at exactly who these people are. Agents generally don't read unsolicited manuscripts, and many editors of nonfiction don't either. But few fiction editors won't read unsolicited work, and virtually all of these fall into two categories: certain editors at large book publishers, and fiction editors at half a dozen of the most prestigious commercial magazines.

But these editors don't buy *any* material not submitted by a reputable literary agent—or by a writer they know personally. Querying these people, then, is pointless. While some of these editors do officially read queries, and even occasionally respond to them with, "Yes, please let me see it," in practice they never actually *buy* manuscripts submitted by writers they're not already familiar with. If you want to sell to one of these editors, you need an agent.

How do you know which editors read unsolicited fiction and which ones do not? Here is an excellent rule of thumb: assume that adult mainstream editors at large book publishers do not, and that all other editors who consider fiction do. If you follow this guideline, you'll be right 95 percent of the time.

Market notices in writers' magazines and listings in market directories often suggest or insist that writers query first, even on fiction. *Ignore these instructions whenever you see them.* Many editors publicly ask writers to query first simply to avoid being inundated by unsolicited work; but most of these editors do in fact read unsolicited material. Again, the only exceptions are certain editors at major book publishers and the largest commercial magazines; as we have seen, there is no point in querying these people at all.

It *is* possible—though quite rare—that you may send in an unsolicited manuscript following the guidelines above, only to have it returned unread with a form letter insisting that you query first. This isn't a rejection; the manuscript hasn't been read at all. Go ahead and write a query letter, following the guidelines on pages 124-130; if you get a positive response, you can then send the manuscript right back.

Book packagers do not normally need to be queried regarding fiction. If you do not know whether a packager considers fiction submissions, however, it is a good idea to call first and ask. If a book packager *does* return an unsolicited manuscript unread and asks you to query first (unlikely but possible), you can then write a query letter following the quidelines on pages 124-130.

WRITERS' GUIDELINES

Many publications and presses issue what are called *writers' guidelines* or *spec sheets*. These are brief descriptions of what sort of material a publisher is looking for, and instructions on how to write for one or more of its columns, features, magazines, or lines or series of books.

These guidelines are available to writers on request, at no charge. You may make your request by mail or phone. If you use the mail, enclose a self-addressed #10 stamped envelope (or, if the publisher is in another country, an envelope and International Reply Coupon). If you use the phone, begin by asking for either the editorial department or the editor in charge of the appropriate department, magazine, genre, or series.

Most commercial magazines and book publishers issue writers' guidelines; most literary magazines and presses do not. I have found that spec sheets from most publishers are only somewhat helpful; like listings in writers' magazines and market directories, they can be vague, misleading, and even downright false. Length limits in particular may be misrepresented. You will always get a better feel for what an editor wants by doing market research than by reading a spec sheet; in fact, when your research contradicts a publisher's own guidelines, believe your research and not the guidelines.

There are three very important exceptions to this rule, however. The following publications normally publish excellent, accurate, and very helpful spec sheets: genre magazines; lines or series of genre books; and other lines or series of books with clearly targeted audiences—e.g., Christian inspirational novels for 9–12-year-olds. In these cases, the publisher is usually seeking a very specific type of material. Length, style, characters, setting, and even some elements of the plot may be strictly predetermined; to sell to such a market you may have to tailor your work to the publisher's specifications. A spec sheet will tell you exactly what limits you must stay within and what remains entirely up to you. If you are interested in writing for such a magazine or ongoing series, I strongly recommend that you order writers' guidelines before submitting your work—and perhaps before writing it.

SIMULTANEOUS SUBMISSIONS

When you send the same manuscript to more than one editor or book packager at a time, it is known as a *simultaneous* or *multiple submission*. Some *nonfiction* editors discourage simultaneous submissions, or refuse to read them at all. However, simultaneous submission is the rule for fiction.

Indeed, I urge you to circulate 3-5 copies of any manuscript at once, and for book proposals I suggest 3-12 copies. The more editors that are looking at a piece at once, the more likely you are to sell it, and the sooner an offer to publish it is likely to come. It is *not* necessary—or desirable—to tell any editor or packager that your manuscript is also in other people's hands when you make your submission. If a market notice or listing says, "no simultaneous submissions," *multiply submit the piece anyway*.

But what if two editors are interested in the same piece? Let's look at all possible scenarios. Suppose you send copies of your story, "Shootout at the Kyoto Temple," to editors at four magazines. After a few weeks, the editor at *Buddhist Cowboy* offers to buy the piece. Are you in any kind of trouble?

No, you're not. Simply write a short, polite withdrawal letter to each of the other three editors; do this immediately, of course. You do not need to explain *why* you are withdrawing the piece.

The matter is now completely taken care of. No editor will be angry or upset, and you've done nothing legally or morally wrong. (See sample withdrawal letter on page 71.)

Note that the sample letter does several things in addition to withdrawing the original manuscript: it maintains a friendly contact with the editor; it reasserts my interest in the magazine; it offers the editor something to make up for my withdrawal; and it alerts the editor to my future submission of another piece.

If you do offer a substitute manuscript, don't send it with your letter of withdrawal; the editor may assume that the letter is a cover letter without reading it, and may put both the manuscript and letter aside to be read at a later date. Send the withdrawal letter promptly, and (if you wish) follow it up with another submission a few days or weeks later.

What if the worst happens, and two different editors simultaneously offer to publish the same piece? Or if one editor offers to publish a piece, you accept the offer and send out withdrawal letters, and, before your letters have arrived, another editor offers to publish the same piece?

First of all, the chances of this happening are very close to zero. It's never happened to me, or to any writer I know. If this extraordinarily unlikely situation does happen to you, simply write or call the editor who lost out on getting your manuscript. Explain honestly what happened and apologize. Offer to send the editor another of your pieces as a possible replacement. The editor may be disappointed, but its unlikely that he or she will be angry with you. In any case, the simultaneous exposure of your work to many different editors has been more than worth this very small risk.

One thing you must *not* do is try to play one offer against the other. If the editor at *Buddhist Cowboy* wants to publish your story, don't call the editor at *Zen Roundup* and say, "I've got an offer of $300 from another magazine. Would you like to top it?" Literary agents can occasionally set up such impromptu auctions on books; but as individual authors, you and I have neither the right nor the power to do this. (If you *do* try it, you may anger both editors, and both may choose not to publish your piece, or anything else you write.)

2706 West 43 Street, Suite 102
Minneapolis, MN 55410
(612) 929-9123

August 11, 1990

Ms. Karen Krystal
Fiction Editor, <u>Buddhist Cowboy</u>
20 Anytown Road
Mainstreet, WI 53222

Dear Karen Krystal:

On June 29 I sent you a copy of my most recent short story,
"Shootout at the Kyoto Temple." Unfortunately, I must withdraw
this piece from your consideration. Please return it to me at
your convenience.

I am at work on another story that I believe you'll enjoy,
however, and will get it off to you once it's finished.

Thank you. All best wishes.

Sincerely,

Scott Edelstein

The above discussion presumes that you have offered the same unpublished manuscript to editors interested in reaching similar audiences. If the piece has already been published and you are selling reprint rights, or if the publications in question have different readerships, then there is probably no conflict that needs to be resolved at all.

Once a short piece has already been published, it can usually be sold again and again, though of course only to publications that use reprints. A publisher that purchases reprint rights to a piece rarely cares where else it is being published; indeed, most publishers that reprint material purchase nonexclusive reprint rights, which means that any other publisher may publish the same piece at any time.

Now let's presume once again that your manuscript (of any length) *hasn't* been published, and editors in both the U.S. and England offer to publish it. In most cases, there is no conflict here: you can sell first North American rights to the first publisher and first British Commonwealth rights to the second.

Or suppose that the editors of two newspaper supplements, one in California and another in Minnesota, want to publish the same shorter piece. Simply call both editors and explain the situation. Since very few people read both supplements, it's very likely that both editors will still want to use your piece, and neither will mind the other's publication.

Is there any limit on the number of submissions you may make simultaneously? Not really. But, except for book proposals, sending out more than half a dozen copies at once probably isn't cost-effective.

Are there any situations in which you simply shouldn't make multiple submissions at all? Yes, there are a few:

● Don't send the same piece simultaneously to more than one newspaper in the same metropolitan area. Newspapers sometimes rush pieces into print, occasionally before notifying writers that their work has been accepted. You don't want two competing newspapers publishing your piece at the same time. (It *is* perfectly acceptable to simultaneously submit the same manuscript to newspapers in two different metropolitan areas.)

• Don't send the same manuscript simultaneously to two different editors at the same publication or book publisher. This is considered both pushy and unprofessional. However, if an editor who rejects your manuscript later leaves his or her job, you may then resubmit the piece to that same press or publication. (This strategy often works. Writer Eric Heideman, for example, had a short story rejected by *Alfred Hitchcock's Mystery Magazine*. A few years later, when a new editor took over, Heideman sent her the same story. The new editor bought it—and the piece went on to win the Robert L. Fish award and a place in a "year's best" anthology.)

• If you sign a publishing contract with a book publisher that includes an option clause requiring you to show that publisher your next book or proposal before showing it to editors at other houses, you must of course keep this promise. In general, though, I urge you to try to negotiate the removal of the option clause from any publishing contract when you first work out a deal.

• If you feel quite confident that a certain editor will offer to purchase a particular piece for an acceptable price, then multiply submitting that piece is both pointless and counterproductive. I should add, however, that I can think of only two circumstances in which such confidence is justified: 1) if the editor has bought most or all of the fiction you have sent him or her before, or 2) if you are so well known (at least in the appropriate genre) that the value of your name alone makes whatever you write salable.

MULTIPLE MANUSCRIPTS

When submitting your work to an editor or book packager, how many different manuscripts should you send at once?

Most writers send no more than one story, novella, book, or book proposal to the same person at a time. This keeps the editor from feeling overwhelmed or put-upon.

There are no hard-and-fast rules about this, however. One writer I know always submits two of her stories to editors at a time, on the grounds that this gives them the choice of one piece or the other instead of simply yes or no. This has evidently worked for her, as well as for other writers.

My own experience, however, and that of many other writers I know, has been that sending one piece at a time usually yields better results. Sometimes, in fact, when an editor is faced with two pieces by the same writer, he or she will rush through both of them and make a hasty (and usually negative) decision. When given only one manuscript, however, that same editor is more likely to take his or her time.

There *are* some situations in which it makes sense to send more than one manuscript at a time:

- When an editor, book packager, agent, or other publishing professional has specifically asked you to send two or more pieces.
- When you are submitting very short work. Pieces of 2,000 words or less may be submitted in pairs; manuscripts of 1,500 words or less can be sent in groups of three.
- When you are submitting the text for short children's books (those running twenty manuscript pages or less). You may send two or at most three of these at a time, up to about fifty pages. If you are including the complete artwork for a book, however, send only one book at a time. (If you're sending text and only *samples* of artwork, you may submit multiple manuscripts.)

If you do send more than one piece to an editor, packager, or agent at once, it's all right to enclose a single return envelope.

It is perfectly acceptable to send a short manuscript to a magazine or newspaper editor, then to send a second piece after about three weeks, even if the editor hasn't responded to the first piece. You may do this again a few weeks later; but three pieces under consideration at once is the limit. With book editors and packagers, standard procedure is to wait for a reply to one submission before making another.

If you are proposing a series to an editor or packager, your proposal should include a description of the series, but no more than one manuscript or novel proposal. If you have already completed other books or novel proposals for the series, say so in your cover letter or series proposal.

PERSISTENCE

Until and unless you become famous, your work will probably be rejected far more often than it will be accepted. Most of what I write gets rejected repeatedly before I sell it, and it took me many years to become a full-time freelance writer.

If you have faith in a piece, keep sending it out until you sell it. I know of stories and books that have been rejected dozens of times — in some cases over a hundred times — before finally being accepted by reputable publishers. And I know writers who have had dozens of pieces rejected by the same editor before that editor finally said, "I'd like to buy this one." Persistence is one of the keys to acceptance and success.

This doesn't mean you shouldn't revise a piece that needs work, or file away one that you feel doesn't deserve publication. It *does* mean sticking with any piece that you feel deserves to be published.

GENERAL TIPS ON APPROACHING EDITORS

One of the best ways to present work to an editor is to have it recommended by someone that editor knows and respects: another editor, someone else in publishing, another writer, or even a friend, relative, or neighbor. An even better way is to have that person deliver or present your work directly to the editor for you. Chapter 8 explains in detail how to make and most effectively use those personal and professional contacts.

Some literary magazines accept submissions only during certain months of the year. This period can be anywhere from 3 to 10 months long. When researching literary magazines, read the small print on the first few pages of a recent issue; if the magazine limits the times during which it accepts submissions, it will say so here.

A very few literary magazines and presses charge writers a reading fee simply to have their work considered for publication. This can range from $1 for a short story to $10 for a book-length manuscript. I find such fees abhorrent, and urge writers to avoid submitting their work to publishers that charge them.

Both for easy reference and to avoid confusion, keep careful, accurate records of all submissions. Each time you send out a manuscript, note the date, the editor's name, and the name of the publication or press. If the manuscript is rejected, note the date on which you receive it back. When you sell the piece, note the date, the price paid, the rights sold, and the terms of the sale. Hang onto all of these records indefinitely.

CHECKLIST

Essential guidelines for approaching editors:
- Always write to editors by name, not merely by title.
- Don't query editors about fiction manuscripts. Either send your work unsolicited, arrange a referral through a contact, or get an agent to represent it. Write a query *only* if your manuscript is returned unread with a note insisting that you query first.
- If you have (or wish to write) a genre book, or material for a genre magazine, request writers' guidelines from the appropriate publishers. Also request guidelines if you wish to submit a book for an ongoing line or series.
- You may normally send the same piece to several different editors at once. Exceptions are noted on pages 72-73.
- If an editor makes an offer to publish a piece and you accept that offer, immediately contact any other editors to whom you have submitted it. Either withdraw the manuscript or explain the situation.
- With the exceptions of very short pieces and brief children's books, submit only one manuscript to an editor

at a time — unless you are specifically asked to do otherwise.

- Keep careful, accurate records of all submissions.

CHAPTER 6

APPROACHING
AGENTS

CHAPTER 3 OF THIS BOOK gave you step-by-step instructions for locating agents. In this chapter I'll show you how to best make contact with agents, and how to tell from their responses which ones are worth working with.

Although most agents in North America who handle fiction live in or near New York City, there are some very effective agents throughout the continent, both in large cities and (in a few cases) small towns. Like members of other professions, agents range from extremely helpful to useless, and from scrupulously honest to thoroughly crooked.

Remember that an agent who might be perfect for one writer might be of no use to another. One mystery writer I know had two different agents over the course of two years; neither was able to sell her first two books. After getting rid of both ineffective agents, she signed on with a third, who almost immediately sold both of her books to a major press. (Those two "ineffective" agents, incidentally, have proven highly effective for other writers.)

Agents make a living by taking a portion of the money their writers earn in commissions. Most agents take 15 percent (a few take 10 percent) of the money a book earns through North American sales, and 20-25 percent on foreign sales and the sale of rights to TV and film producers. (The commission on these sales is higher because a second agent, called a subagent, is involved.)

No decent agent takes commissions in excess of these. Furthermore, you should never have to pay any agent a fee for reading or submitting your work. Nor should you have to reimburse an agent for expenses, with the exception of certain photocopying costs and other *small occasional* expenses.

GETTING STARTED

You may initially approach agents by mail, by phone, or through a personal or professional contact. In general, I recommend not using the phone unless you are an absolute master at telephone selling and conversation, because fiction books are usually very difficult to synopsize and present verbally.

You may write as many query letters to agents at a time as you wish (5-10 is a good range); use the guidelines in Chapter 10 to write the best, most professional query you can. An excellent example of a query letter to agents appears on pages 128-129. Be sure to write directly to a particular agent, not just to an agency. That is, don't write to the George Lundquist Agency (unless George is its only agent). Instead, write to Marlene Stoffels at the George Lundquist Agency.

You may introduce either one or two projects in your query letter—no more. If you have others, wait until you receive a response from the agent before mentioning them.

You may use the same text for all your query letters, but each letter should be freshly typed; don't use a photocopied form letter. Enclose a stamped, self-addressed business envelope for the agent's reply.

Never send an agent an unsolicited manuscript unless a listing in one of the directories listed on pages 26-27 specifically states that the agent reads unsolicited material. Even then, an initial query is often a better idea.

Responses to your query letter should begin to come in (some by phone, most by mail) within a couple of weeks. Each agent will respond in one of three ways: 1) by asking to see the manuscript(s); 2) by declining to look at the manuscript(s); or 3) by offering to read or submit the manuscript(s) in exchange for a fee, usually between $50 and $350.

Under no circumstances should you ever have to pay any such fee. It is through these fees, and not through commissions on sales, that many second-rate agents make much or most of their money. Some quite reputable agents charge reading fees, too, but will sometimes waive them at a writer's request. So if you are asked to pay a reading fee, don't automatically toss the agent's letter in the garbage. *If* the agent impresses or appeals to you, or has been highly recommended, you may wish to politely write or call him or her. Explain that you appreciate his or her interest in your work, and say that you'd like to send it, but that you would like the reading fee waived. If the agent is legitimate, and seriously interested in your work, he or she will probably waive the fee.

Some agents who charge reading fees call them critiquing fees, and will give you both a reading and a critique. (One large literary agency does a thriving business in these critiques. I've seen one of them, and it was awful.) But even if you're offered a critique and a free toaster, don't agree to pay a fee. Some so-called agents may also offer to rewrite your work to make it more "salable" for an additional fee. The only sane response to this offer is a firm no.

Once an agent has asked to read your work, send it, along with a brief letter, via first class or priority mail — or, if the agent is in another country, via airmail. Your letter should thank the agent for his or her interest in your project(s) and *very briefly* reintroduce the material you've enclosed. Add a return envelope or mailing bag and sufficient postage (or, if appropriate, International Reply Coupons) for the material's return.

You may send your work to only one North American agent at a time. If two or more agents ask to see your material, send it to the agent who interests you most. If this agent turns down your work, or if he or she likes it but you decide you'd rather be represented by someone else, you can then (and only then) send it to another agent. In such circumstances, apologize to the second agent for taking so long to send your work, but don't explain the cause of the delay. If necessary, repeat this process with other agents. (You *may* send your work to two or more agents simultaneously *if* they are in different countries. For example, you may send material to an agent in the U.S. for representation in North America, and at the same time send the same work to an agent in Paris for representation in France.)

If an agent hasn't replied to your query at all within two months, forget about him or her. You don't want someone this slow or thoughtless representing you. However, if the agent later responds positively, and provides a good explanation for his or her tardiness (a serious illness, a trip abroad, etc.), then you should of course have no qualms about sending your work. "I've been very busy," however, is not an acceptable excuse; an agent too busy to respond to a query within a reasonable time will be too busy to adequately represent you.

Sometimes, even though you have finished a manuscript, an agent will ask to see only portions of it; if he or she likes those portions, the agent will then ask to see the rest of the book. Or the agent may ask to see a proposal instead of the completed book. You can deal with this second request in one of three ways:

- Create a proposal, working backward from your finished novel, and send it off.
- Send the finished book, along with a polite note explaining that the novel is complete and that no proposal is available.
- Call the agent to discuss the situation. Explain that no proposal is available, and ask to be permitted to send the completed book. It's possible that the agent misread your letter, and believed that you had completed a proposal instead of a finished novel. It's also quite possible that he or she typed "proposal" instead of "book" out of sheer habit. A quick phone call can straighten this out quickly.

Some writers have encountered the opposite situation, in which they've written only a proposal but the agent requests a finished book. If this happens to you, either send the agent your proposal, along with a note explaining that the proposal is all that's available, or give the agent a polite call to discuss the situation.

Most agents will take 3-6 weeks to read your material; some may take longer. Three months, however, is too long; once an agent has had your work for this long, politely call or write to request your material back. This agent is too slow, or too busy, to be effective for you.

After the agent has read your material, he or she will either offer to represent it, return it to your with a letter declining it, or request a rewrite. Treat rewrite requests from agents just as you would similar requests from editors.

ARRANGING REPRESENTATION

Once an agent offers to represent your work, don't automatically say yes. First ask some pointed questions:

- What are some of the fiction projects you've sold *in the past year*? Which publishers did you sell them to? (If you have a genre book, ask about recent sales in that genre.)
- What is your commission on domestic sales? On foreign sales? On other sales where subagents are involved?
- Do you charge fees of any kind?
- Do you have affiliated agents who handle foreign rights for you? TV and film rights?
- Do you sign a written agreement with your clients, or do you simply make oral agreements? What are the basic terms of this agreement?

Do not become a client of any North American agent unless he or she has sold at least a few fiction titles (or, if your book is a genre book, at least a few titles in that genre) *within the past year or so to major U.S. publishers*. This holds true whether the agent is American or Canadian, and whether you live in the U.S., Canada, or elsewhere. You do *not* want or need someone with good intentions and a poor (or no) sales record. You need an agent who is able to sell the kind of book or proposal you have written, and can sell it to a house that can publish and promote it well throughout the continent. Foreign agents should have similar sales records in their own territories.

While it's always a plus if an agent has affiliates who handle film, TV, or foreign rights, it isn't a necessity. As for oral vs.

written agreements, it doesn't matter which the agent uses so long as the terms of your agreement are quite clear. If you do make only an oral agreement, I strongly suggest going over the terms together, and writing them down for your own later reference.

Whether your agreement is oral or written, don't agree to any unreasonable terms; unfortunately, some otherwise decent agents may offer them. Here are some things to watch for, and to negotiate if necessary:

● A good agent works on a project-by-project basis. Don't make an agreement that allows an agent to represent everything (or every book and book proposal) you write.

● A good agent doesn't want money he or she didn't earn. Don't let your agent take a percentage of whatever money you make from your writing, including money from deals you made without his or her assistance. The agent should only be entitled to a commission on sales he or she made.

● Publishers will pay your agent, who will deduct the agent's commission and pay you the remainder. These payments should be made to you within a month of the agent's receipt of any payment from a publisher.

● Avoid letting an agent represent your work for a fixed period of time — e.g., for one or two years. Ideally, either you or your agent should be able to terminate your relationship by simply giving 30-90 days' notice to the other party. If an agent insists on representing you for a fixed period of time, however, a six-month period is reasonable.

● Try to get rid of any "next work" provision from your agreement. This would give the agent the right to represent your next book or proposal, no matter what kind of a job he or she does with the current one. At the very least, try to change "next work" to "next work in the same genre," or "next young adult novel," or simply "next fiction book."

With a little luck, eventually you and your agent will come to an agreement. He or she will then ask for 2-3 additional copies of your finished book, or 2-10 additional copies of your proposal.

(A good agent sends out at least three copies of a finished book at once, and at least four copies of a proposal.) If your agent *doesn't* ask for these multiple copies, bring up the subject yourself. Send the requested number of copies promptly; make sure they are clear, dark, complete, and in excellent condition.

One alternative you have is to ask the agent to make the photocopies for you and to bill you for their cost. This is standard practice — so standard that some agents automatically do the photocopying and don't even bother to ask authors to send copies. Pay any photocopying bill promptly.

Once you have agreed on the terms of representation, you should provide your agent with the following information:

- The names of anyone you know who works in book publishing, especially those who have expressed interest in your work. Explain how you know them, the nature of your relationship, what their jobs are, and what publishers they work for. Also mention the names and employers of any magazine editors you know who may be interested in serializing your book or running an excerpt from it.

- What portions of your manuscript, if any, have already been sold or published, and when and where they appeared (or will appear). This includes any material you may have self-published.

- The names of all editors and presses, if any, that have already seen and rejected your project. If the manuscript has been substantially revised at any point, list only rejections that occurred after this revision.

- A complete list of your major publications, sales, credentials, and relevant background information.

OTHER TIPS ON AGENTS

- Once you have established a relationship with an agent, you do not need to query before sending additional manuscripts, and you do not need to enclose return envelopes or return postage with your work. However, don't inundate your agent with material; it's annoying and unprofessional.

• Except as noted earlier, agents rarely critique manuscripts. Nor will they often praise a literary work, even if they like it a great deal.

• If you are represented by Jack Fleischer at the Melanie Malone Literary Agency, your author-agent agreement will be between you and the Malone Agency. In practice, however, Jack Fleischer will be completely and solely responsible for representing your work.

• Some North American literary agents have a network of subagents throughout the world; some have few or no such affiliations. For every country, territory, or language in which your North American agent does not provide representation, you have the right to seek representation from a foreign agent on your own. You should approach foreign agents just as you would agents in North America. Write your query letter in English unless you are fluent in the appropriate language; manuscripts should normally be submitted in English as well. Explain in your letter that you already have North American representation; mention your agent's name and the name of the agency.

• If an editor makes an offer on a book or proposal that you're submitting on your own, and you realize you want an agent to negotiate the deal for you, don't agree to *any* terms of the editor's offer. Just note them down and promise to get back in touch within a few days. Then, using the tips in Chapter 3, make a list of agents to contact, and begin *calling* them — there is no time for letters. Explain that you have an offer from a press and need someone to negotiate it for you. It shouldn't be hard to get an agent under these circumstances, provided there's a reasonable chunk of money in it for the agent. However, if you are offered an advance of less than $1,500, or no advance at all, you may have some trouble getting an agent interested, since there will be little or no commission money involved. Some agents do negotiate contracts on a noncommission basis for writers who are not their clients, usually for about $50 an hour. Ask about this if you are having trouble finding an agent who will represent you on a commission basis. Some agents will also provide advice on contract negotiation to nonclients, again usually for about $50 an hour. Some of the agents who provide these services are noted in the Author's Agents section of *Writer's Market*.

- If you try to get an agent to represent a project and cannot, don't despair. You can always seek representation again — even from the same agents you have already contacted — for your next manuscript. In the meantime, use the other chapters in this book to market your current project yourself.

- For an excellent and more detailed look at agents, consult Michael Larsen's *Literary Agents: How to Get and Work with the Right One for You* (Writer's Digest Books).

CHECKLIST

Basic procedures for approaching agents:
- Always write to a particular agent by name, not merely to an agency.
- Unless you know someone who can introduce you and your work to an agent, make your initial contact through a query letter. You may query as many agents at once as you wish. Do not send unsolicited material.
- You may send a manuscript to only one agent in North America at a time.
- Never pay a reading or critiquing fee. If an agent asks for such a fee, either ask him or her to waive it or ask for your manuscript back.
- If an agent offers to represent your work, don't immediately say yes. First ask the important questions on page 82.
- Don't work with an agent who has made few or no recent fiction sales (or sales in the same genre as your project) to major U.S. publishers.
- Find out precisely what an agent's terms of representation will be, and negotiate them if necessary. Come to a clear agreement. This may be either written or oral; if it is oral, review the terms with the agent and write them down.

- Your agent's commissions should not exceed 15 percent on domestic rights and 25 percent on foreign, TV, and film rights.
- Make sure your agent sends out at least three copies of each project (at least four for book proposals) to editors simultaneously. Either send your agent these copies promptly or reimburse him or her for the cost of making them for you.
- Let your agent know the names, job titles, and employers of anyone you know in book publishing; the names of editors and presses that have previously rejected your manuscript; and when and where portions of your manuscript have been previously published, if such is the case.
- Once you have established a relationship with an agent, you do not need to query on future projects, nor do you need to send return envelopes and return postage. Simply send the new material with a cover letter.

CHAPTER 7

LOOKING YOUR BEST

YOU KNOW ALREADY HOW IMPORTANT IT IS for each of your manuscripts and business letters to look neat, polished, and as professional as possible. But it's at least as important that you, the writer, also look skilled and professional. This is particularly true when you wish to sell a novel proposal, because you are asking editors to invest not in a finished product but in your ability as a writer.

This chapter will show you how and when to best present supporting materials and information to people in publishing, and how to make yourself look as good as possible.

LISTING YOUR CREDENTIALS AND BACKGROUND

When you approach an editor, book packager, agent, or other publishing professional, one (and no more than one) paragraph of your cover or query letter should be devoted to listing your publications and other appropriate credentials, background, and/or experience. In the case of books and book proposals, you should provide this information in your author biography as well.

It is essential that you present information about yourself in a concise and straightforward manner. Don't write an ad for yourself or attempt a hard sell. Simply present the pertinent facts in a way that publishing people will find most impressive.

Here, for example, is what I typically say in a cover letter accompanying an unsolicited short story submission to a general-interest magazine:

> I've been publishing short stories since 1972, and my fiction and nonfiction have appeared in over twenty magazines, ranging from *Glamour* and *Artlines* to *Ellery Queen's Mystery Magazine* and *City Miner*. I've also published several books with Harper & Row, Bantam, Lyle Stuart, and other major publishers.

This paragraph, while obviously intended to impress, is factual from beginning to end. Nowhere have I praised or flattered myself. Yet my subtext is, "I've published widely and in respectable places for nearly two decades, and thus am an experienced and talented professional." Were I to overtly sing my own praises ("I'm considered one of the brightest young writers in the Upper Midwest, etc.") I would sound arrogant, silly, and amateurish—and editors would react negatively.

Although you should carefully avoid such a sales pitch, it's nevertheless important that you present any information about yourself in as favorable a factual light as possible.

Let's use imaginary writer Barbara Gross as an example. Barbara has published four pieces: a poem in a local literary magazine, a book review in the Houston *Post*, a short story in *The Magazine of Fantasy and Science Fiction*, and a short essay in *Chicago Review*. These publications are nothing to sneeze at; but note that only one of them is a piece of fiction. Here's what Barbara might write in a cover letter accompanying the submission of a short story to a literary magazine:

> My previous work has been published in several national and regional publications, including *Chicago Review*. My most recent piece, "At Work," appeared in the literary magazine *Local Hero*.

By playing up her publications in literary magazines and referring to her book review, essay, and poem as "previous work,"

Barbara has put the best possible spin on her publications.

Whom you are writing to will often determine what information you present and how you present it. For example, suppose Barbara decides to send her newest story not to a literary magazine, but to the science fiction magazine *Analog*. Here's how the biographical material in her cover letter might read:

> My previous work has appeared in several national and regional publications. My most recent publications include the story "Hours Away," in *The Magazine of Fantasy and Science Fiction*.

Here again Barbara's poem, essay, and review have become simply "previous work." Because the editor at *Analog* is likely to be impressed by other science fiction and fantasy publications, but not by publications in literary magazines, she has mentioned only *The Magazine of Fantasy and Science Fiction* by name.

All of this means figuring out who will be most impressed by what. An editor at *Yankee*, for example, is likely to be impressed by publications in many commercial and literary magazines. On the other hand, the *Yankee* editor will be *unfavorably* impressed by publications in *Screw* or in a local avant-garde literary tabloid called *Sophisticated Puke*. An editor at *The Kenyon Review* will be impressed by publication in any large or medium-sized literary magazine, either regional or national (e.g., *Ohio Review, Cream City Review, Cimarron Review*, etc.), but not by publication in *Alfred Hitchcock's Mystery Magazine* or children's magazines. No editors at all will be impressed by your publications in your neighborhood newspaper, your self-published chapbook, or your letter to the editor in *Harper's*.

There is sometimes a fine line between what constitutes publication and what does not. If you sell a 1,000-word "Humor in Uniform" piece to *Reader's Digest*, you may legitimately claim that your work has appeared in that magazine. But publication of a letter to the editor or a *Playboy* party joke is *not* considered publication of your work.

When discussing your background and credentials, you should list not only publications, but pieces that have been accepted but not yet published; these pieces are said to be "forthcoming" or "scheduled for publication."

If you are sending a piece to a literary magazine or press, or to a nongenre magazine that specializes in fiction, you may mention any *graduate* degrees you've earned in *creative writing* (*not* in English, literature, or other kinds of writing). If you're currently enrolled in a graduate creative writing program, say so. And if you studied (or are currently studying) under someone well known, you might write, for example, "I'm currently working toward my M.F.A. at the University of British Columbia, where I'm studying with Herman Melville."

If you were or are a stringer or journalist for a large or medium-sized magazine or newspaper, this is worth mentioning to editors at commercial publications and presses. If you were or are a staff writer or editor for a publication or press, this is also worth mentioning.

Also mention any nonwriting background that may have a bearing on your submission. For instance, if your story is set in a research station in Antarctica, and you spent six months living in such a station, definitely say so. (Don't go on and on about it, however; one or two sentences will do.)

If you have no publishing credentials or background worth mentioning, don't mention any. Avoid the subject entirely.

LISTING ORGANIZATIONAL AFFILIATIONS

If you are a member of one or more organizations of professional writers, it may be worth noting your membership(s) on certain manuscripts. This depends on the nature of the organization, the type of material you're submitting, and the editor, book packager, or agent to whom you are submitting the piece.

Only list your membership in organizations that have a publication requirement for joining. Do not indicate your membership in writers' clubs, writers' centers, or the National Writers' Union. To say that you're a member of one of these organizations doesn't tell editors that you're a pro; it only tells them that you've paid the organization your annual dues. But if you're a member (for example) of Mystery Writers of America or the Authors Guild, it means you're a published pro.

Once again you should bear in mind who will be impressed by what information. Don't mention your membership in Western Writers of America unless you are submitting a western. If you have a highly literate suspense story that you're submitting to a literary magazine, you're probably better off not mentioning your membership in Mystery Writers of America. But you *should* list this affiliation if you send that same piece to *Alfred Hitchcock's Mystery Magazine*.

Organizational affiliations should be listed only on manuscripts, not in cover letters, query letters, or author biographies. Indicate your affiliation simply by typing "Member, _____." This belongs two lines below your telephone number(s), on either the first page of your short manuscript or the cover page of your book or book proposal. If you wish to list more than one affiliation, type the second immediately below the first; do not skip a line in between.

Listing an organizational affiliation is most helpful when you are a member of a genre writers' organization and are submitting work to a magazine or line of books in that genre.

AUTHOR BIOGRAPHIES

A standard part of most book manuscripts and proposals is a one-page (or shorter) author biography. As with cover and query letters, this should make you look as able and experienced as possible. In the case of book proposals, it should also clearly establish you as a reliable professional capable of completing a solid, successful book.

Your author biography may be longer, more informal, and a bit chattier than biographical information in letters. Generally, your author biography should resemble those published on dust jackets and in the backs of books — though, when possible, yours should be longer and more detailed.

Write your biography in the third person present, e.g., "Tamara Cooper is the author of several Harlequin romance novels.

Her newest book, *Autumn Blossoms*, was published by Harlequin in a first printing of 200,000 copies."

A sample biography for imaginary author Walter Wright appears on page 94. This biography is meant to accompany Walter's first novel, *Driven to Murder*. Note that it simultaneously establishes him as a professional mystery writer, a published book author, and an expert on the novel's central theme of automobiles.

Walter sounds in this biography like a solidly established pro. But in eight years of writing, he has published a total of only seven items: three short articles on restoring cars in automotive magazines; three mystery stories, two in mystery magazines and one in a Sunday newspaper supplement; and one nonfiction book with a fairly small publisher. But by presenting these limited credentials in as positive a manner as possible, this biography encourages editors to expect a book that is, at the very least, competently written and worthy of their consideration.

If you have few or no publications or credentials, or little or no appropriate background, you may—and, indeed, should—omit an author biography entirely. However, if you can put together even one three-sentence paragraph, this is a good idea. For example:

> HOWARD GHENT has been writing and publishing since 1978. His work has appeared in the Minneapolis *Star Tribune*, as well as in national publications. *Boardwalk Blues* is his first novel; he is at work on his second, *Losing Ground*.

While this paragraph doesn't make Howard sound like a seasoned professional, at least he doesn't appear to be a novice. In fact, however, he has published only three items in his entire career: a short opinion piece in the *Star Tribune* in 1978, a 500-word article in *The Chronicle of Philanthropy*, and a short poem in *The Writer*.

When preparing your own author biography, begin by typing the heading "About the Author," centered and underlined. Drop down three or four lines and begin your text. The entire biography should be double- or 1½-spaced and vertically cen-

About the Author

WALTER WRIGHT has been publishing both fiction and nonfiction since 1985. His mystery and suspense stories have appeared in <u>Ellery Queen's Mystery Magazine</u>, <u>Hitchcock's Mystery Magazine</u>, and elsewhere, and his short nonfiction has been published in a number of national magazines.

In many of his stories, as in <u>Driven to Murder</u>, Mr. Wright writes about people obsessed with the mystique, power, and dark side of the American automobile. This is only fitting, since Mr. Wright is obsessed with them himself, and has collected and repaired antique cars for over a decade.

<u>Driven to Murder</u> is his second book. His first, <u>Maximum Mileage: How to Make Your Car Last 250,000 Miles</u>, was published in 1988 by the Stephen Greene Press.

Mr. Wright lives with his wife and daughter in Milwaukee, where he is at work on his next mystery novel.

tered on the page. It may be as short as one paragraph, but no more than one page.

Author biographies should be included *only* with books and proposals. For shorter material, include such information only in cover and query letters.

Other tips on writing an effective author biography:

• If a published review of one of your pieces contains an especially good quote, or if someone well known has said or written something quite positive about your work, you may include one or two such *very brief* quotes in your biography. For example, "Mark Twain called Scott Edelstein's last book, *Quivering Adjectives*, 'the best damn thing put between two covers all year,' and Emily Dickinson wrote that Edelstein's work 'can be counted on to help the reader through the longest of Amherst nights.' " These quotes *must* be either from published reviews, writers who are well known (at least within your genre), or non-writers whose names are household words (Willard Scott, Whitney Houston, Jane Pauley, et al.). Although you may list a couple of the best things others have said about your work in an author biography, you may *not* compliment yourself. Just present the facts. Quotes from others constitute facts; self-compliments do not.

• If you have previously sold or published a fiction book, or a nonfiction book for a general audience, by all means mention it. If the book has been successful in some manner — e.g., if it sold lots of copies, had a large first printing, has had a foreign sale, has been optioned for film, etc. — say so. If you can show that one of your previous books has been successful, you'll have an easier time selling your current project.

• If you are at work on another fiction book, or a nonfiction book for a general audience, say so in your biography. This lets editors know that you are more than a one-book writer. You may legitimately say you are working on another book if you are simply making notes on one, or even thinking seriously about one.

• If you are using a pseudonym on your book, your author biography may use your real name, your pen-name, or both, at your discretion.

• If your book is a collaborative effort, your About the Author page should include a short biography for each co-author. Try to fit both on the same page; use 1½ spacing if necessary.

WRITING SAMPLES

Samples of previously published writing can sometimes help sell a book or (especially) a book proposal. Samples are useful in two ways: they serve as examples of your work, and they give editors hard evidence that you are a published professional. By demonstrating that other editors have appreciated your work, they subtly pressure the editor who has received your manuscript to react positively to it.

The fewer publications and other credentials you have, the more helpful one or two samples can be. This is particularly true if you have not previously sold a novel, and/or if you are trying to sell a book proposal. Obviously, you should only enclose samples that you are proud of and that demonstrate your skill as a fiction writer.

If you do include samples, mention in your cover letter that you are doing so. List the samples by title; if they are excerpts from longer works, say so. Also mention when and where they were published. If a piece has been reprinted as well, explain when and where.

Each sample should be clearly photocopied from the published book, magazine, or newspaper in which it appeared. This gives you a psychological edge by showing editors work that has been typeset, printed, and perhaps illustrated as well. Never use manuscript copies. (And *never* submit as samples any material that has gone unsold, or that has been sold but not yet published.) Anything in manuscript form will *look* unpublished — and thus, by inference, unpublishable — even if the facts are otherwise.

The total length of all samples should not exceed twenty-five 8½-by-11-inch photocopied pages; ideally, the length should not exceed fifteen. If you wish to use excerpts, they may be from the same longer work, or from two different ones.

Writing samples should of course relate to the book or proposal you are submitting. If you have a mainstream adult book, your published samples should also be of adult mainstream material; if you have a genre book, your samples should be in the same (or a closely related) genre. If your book or proposal is for young readers, your samples should be for readers in the same age group.

You may enclose samples with submissions to agents just as you would with submissions to editors and book packagers. However, an agent who represents your project will decide whether or not to use the samples when making submissions on your behalf.

Each of your writing samples should be held together with a paper clip. If the samples accompany a proposal, place them in the left-hand pocket of the proposal folder. Do the same for samples accompanying a children's book or other short book. For longer books—those submitted in two-part boxes—place the samples after your author biography.

Include samples of earlier work only with submissions of books or book proposals. Never include samples when submitting shorter works. Samples are, of course, optional. If you don't wish to include them, or if you don't have anything that you feel is appropriate or good enough, omit samples entirely.

REVIEWS

An excellent way to arouse editors' and agents' interest in your book or proposal is to enclose reviews of your work, or quotes therefrom. Obviously, only *highly* positive comments will be useful. If a reviewer calls one of your pieces "entertaining" or "a pleasant read," that's not positive enough; "highly imaginative" or "a very pleasant read" will do, however.

You may present a review in either of two ways: by enclosing a photocopy of the entire review, or by typing the most positive and appropriate passages on a piece of plain paper. Which option you choose depends on the particular review. If one of your previous books has received a highly positive review, a copy of the entire review will be best. If you like, you may neatly circle, underline, or highlight key portions of the review with colored marker. If the name of the reviewer and the title and date of the publication are not clearly indicated, type them on the photocopy. (If a review has been published anonymously, you do not need to find out the author's name.)

If a review is less than enthusiastic, or if it includes more than one or two negative comments, your wisest move is to pick out the most impressive or laudatory quotes. Type them up, 1½- or double-spaced, on a sheet of plain paper. Include the name of the reviewer and the name and date of the publication in which the review appeared. If a review is anonymous, simply attribute the review to the publication itself.

If you wish to quote from more than one review or reviewer, you may put several quotes on the same page. A sample page of quotes appears on page 99.

If you are providing photocopies of complete reviews, they should be appropriate to the book or proposal they accompany. A review of a western novel isn't going to help you sell your mystery, nor is a review of your children's picture book going to impress editors to whom you have submitted your adult novel.

If you assemble a sheet of quotes from reviewers, however, you have more leeway. Look again at the page of quotes for the imaginary writer G.J. Lennox. Since none of these quotes say anything about what type of writing Ms. Lennox does, that page could accompany a book or book proposal of any type. For this reason a page of quotes is often preferable to photocopied reviews.

All reviews and quotes should of course be from reputable publications. Don't use quotes or reviews from your church bulletin or your neighborhood newspaper.

Reviews and/or pages of quotes should only accompany books and proposals — never shorter material. In the case of full-length books, place your reviews and quotations after your author biography and just before your writing samples, if any. In the case of book proposals and short books, place them in the left-hand pocket of your folder; if there are other items in the

Reviews of G.J. Lennox's Work

"Ms. Lennox is a highly talented new writer."

                                        --Booklist, 3/19/92

"One of the most surprising and innovative storytellers I've read
in recent years. G.J. Lennox is worth watching."

                              --Gloria Thomas, Library Journal,
                                April 1992

"Her short story 'Magenta'... is perhaps the best item in the
entire anthology... beautifully written, haunting, and with a
genuinely shocking twist at the end...."

                              --Ted James, The South Coast
                                Review of Books, August 1991

"If Jorge Luis Borges were to have sired an American daughter, her
name would be G.J. Lennox."

                              --Erik Walsh, The Houston Post,
                                9/19/91

pocket, the reviews or page of quotes should be on top of any other pages, but underneath any business envelopes.

ENDORSEMENTS

An endorsement is an *unpublished* quote praising your work from a well-known writer or personality. An endorsement may refer to the project you wish to sell, one or more of your previous projects, or your work in general. Endorsements serve the same purposes as reviews and quotes, with one significant difference: the reputation of the person who makes an endorsement is as important as the praise given you or your work.

Endorsements can be enormously helpful in selling books and book proposals, and in getting agents to represent your material. Indeed, endorsements can sometimes make or break a book. When I was an agent, I was once told by an editor at Doubleday, "I like the proposal you sent me, but I don't think the marketing people here will let us buy it unless you can get some endorsements from famous people." My author secured the endorsements; the book was purchased and published; and the endorsements appeared on the back of the dust jacket. The editor told me later that it was the endorsements that persuaded her marketing colleagues to say yes to the book.

Endorsements for fiction books and proposals may be from well-known writers in the same literary field or genre as your own project; from well-known writers in general; or from well-known personalities in *any* field. If you have a science fiction book, for example, an endorsement from Joanna Russ or Robert Silverberg (two science fiction writers that most regular SF readers will recognize) will be helpful. An endorsement from Stephen King or Danielle Steel will be still more helpful. And if you can get an endorsement from David Letterman or Elizabeth Dole, whose names are household words, you greatly increase the chances of selling your project. The wider recognition an endorser has, the more the endorsement can help you sell your book or proposal.

Why do endorsements carry so much weight? Because they

can be plastered across book covers, dust jackets, ads, and press releases, and because consumers respond to them.

The best and easiest way to secure an endorsement is to already know a well-known writer or other personality. If you don't, however, use the tips in Chapter 8 to get to know a few such people. (Though it is a longshot, you can try sending *brief* samples of your work to well-known strangers, along with a concise, polite letter asking for a brief endorsement.)

An endorsement may be as simple as one sentence ("I highly recommend this book") or as long as a full page. Save any written endorsement you receive; retype it, 1½- or double-spaced, on a piece of plain paper, as in the sample on page 102. If you wish, you may type up several short endorsements on the same page. You may also mix endorsements and quotes from reviews on the same page(s).

If an endorsement is equivocal, or if only portions of it offer sufficiently high praise, you may select only the most quotable excerpts, just as you may from reviews. However, *never* alter what someone has said.

Occasionally someone may be too busy to give you a written endorsement, but will be happy to give you an oral one. This is fine—but it is essential that you write down the endorsement word for word, then mail a typed transcript of it to the endorser, along with a letter asking him or her to check it over and get in touch with you if it is in any way incorrect. You may wish to ask the endorser to sign and return a copy of the transcribed endorsement. This protects you in the event that the endorser later challenges his or her own endorsement.

Sometimes a famous person will be too busy to give you even an oral endorsement, but will have no objection to signing one you've written yourself. This may sound strange, but it is a quite common practice. If you are asked to write your own endorsement, don't be lengthy or effusive. Your praise should be straightforward, clear, and reasonably concise—and, of course, highly quotable. You *must* send a typed copy of the endorsement to the endorser, along with a letter asking him or her to sign and return the endorsement if it is acceptable. You must have this person's signature to be able to use the endorsement.

G.J. Lennox's <u>Farmer's Market</u> is one of the most unusual and entertaining novels I've read in some time. The prose shimmers; the characters both convince and surprise in every scene. The plot continually takes unexpected turns which nevertheless seem absolutely appropriate. By page fifty, I had given up any hope of second-guessing the plot, and let myself be taken on a bumpy but highly satisfying literary joyride.

                                        Edgar Allan Poe

For proposals, children's books, and other very short books, place any endorsement(s) in the left-hand pocket of your folder, before any writing samples, and either before or after any reviews or quotes. For boxed manuscripts, endorsements belong after your author biography—again, before any writing samples, and either before or after reviews or quotes.

Endorsements are primarily used to sell books and book proposals. There is nothing wrong with including them with shorter manuscripts, but they make much less of a difference in selling shorter work, if they may any difference at all. If you do enclose endorsements with a short piece, place them immediately after your cover letter.

CHECKLIST

Ways to make yourself look as talented and professional as possible:

- Include a paragraph on your writing achievements and related background in every cover and query letter.
- List your membership in any professional writers' organization on manuscripts.
- Enclose an author biography, carefully worded to make the most of your experience and credentials, with every book manuscript or proposal.
- Add 1-2 samples of previously published pieces to books and book proposals.
- Secure endorsements from well-known writers, or from famous people in any field.
- Provide favorable quotes on your work from reviews, or provide highlighted copies of the reviews themselves.

CHAPTER 8

USING PERSONAL CONTACTS TO SELL YOUR WORK

THE IMPORTANCE OF CONTACTS

IF YOU TRULY WANT TO MAXIMIZE your chances for publication and success, you should put a significant portion of your marketing energy into locating, making, sustaining, and using important contacts. The more difficult a certain market or field is to break into, the more important making and using contacts becomes.

Contacts can help you professionally by recommending your work to an editor or agent; by recommending an editor, agent, or market to you; by introducing you to an agent, editor, or other publishing professional; by writing an endorsement for your book; by informing you of new markets or changes in policy or personnel at established ones; by reviewing your book; by organizing a reading or book signing; by interviewing you on radio, on TV, or in print; or by putting you in touch with other important contacts.

Obviously, the best and most important contacts you can have are agents and editors. But many people, both in and outside of publishing, can help you professionally as well. Useful contacts can be bookstore owners and managers, publishing employees other than editors (marketing people, editors' secretaries, etc.), librarians, past or present writing teachers, staff people at writers' centers, friends, acquaintances, relatives, and of course other writers.

Part of what makes contacts work is simple familiarity. If a manuscript arrives on an editor's or agent's desk from a stranger, it's just a stack of papers to be read and judged. But suppose the editor or agent has met you, or talked with you on the phone, or corresponded with you for some time, or had your work recommended by someone he or she knows. Suddenly you are no longer a stranger, but another human being. The stack of pages has become a form of personal communication, not just a collection of words.

Personal and professional contacts cannot work miracles. They will rarely, if ever, enable you to publish badly written fiction. Yet it *is* true that whom you know can be as important, or almost as important, as what you write. Knowing the right people can help you get your work read more promptly, carefully, and sympathetically, and it can get your work read by more of the right people. Indeed, it is often the case that knowing the right person can make the difference between selling a well-written piece and having it rejected.

None of this means that you must know important people in publishing to succeed as a fiction writer. It *is* possible to build a successful writing career without knowing anyone at first. But the more influential people you know, the better your chances for success become, the sooner that success is likely to arrive, and the greater that success is likely to be. If you are a hard-core loner, you can still be published and even become successful. But understand that the odds for success will be slimmer for you than for writers who are willing to spend time building up a network of useful contacts.

MAKING CONTACTS

Making contacts doesn't necessarily mean attending readings, writers' conferences, and literary parties. It certainly *doesn't* mean flattering people indiscriminately or following them around. In fact, one of the biggest benefits of being a writer is that you can make many (or even all) of your contacts by using the phone and the mail.

To some degree, every writer naturally makes and builds

on contacts. For example, every editor who agrees to publish your work becomes a resource you can draw on for information, advice, and referrals. The trick is to use each of your contacts wisely and appropriately to benefit your writing career.

The very best contact a writer of book-length fiction can have is a good literary agent. A good agent knows many of the right people and can use these contacts to sell your work and help you build your career. Many writers have become published and successful on the basis of this one important contact.

But even if you have an agent, it pays to cultivate other contacts. This very book came about because of contacts I built up on my own—contacts my agent didn't have. If I had let my agent manage my entire career, this book wouldn't exist, and I'd be thousands of dollars poorer.

Your most useful contacts are the people you already know in publishing: editors, other writers, sales representatives for publishers, and so on. If you've published a few stories in *Ellery Queen's Mystery Magazine*, for example, and you've just finished your first mystery novel, there may be no better person to contact than *Ellery Queen*'s editor, who might be able to supply you with the names of book editors and/or agents who are looking for mysteries. She might even be willing to recommend your work to one or more of these people. And she might also be able to give you some inside information on each person, e.g., "He drives a hard bargain but likes to buy first novels," "She loves locked-room mysteries," etc.

Of course, most of the people you know personally and professionally probably aren't in publishing. Yet a surprisingly large percentage of these people will have publishing contacts of their own whom they can perhaps put you in touch with. Your dentist may have a brother who's an editor at Harper & Row. The secretary down the hall may be dating a sales rep for Henry Holt. Your veterinarian may go golfing with the person who edits the Sunday supplement for your city's newspaper. This may sound farfetched, but believe me, it isn't. I've found publishing contacts just about everywhere.

Your first step in locating helpful contacts, then, is to make use of the ones you already have. Ask people—your uncle, your secretary, your uncle's secretary, your auto mechanic, your aerobics instructor, the members of your softball team — if they know anyone in writing, publishing, or bookselling. You'll be surprised at how many of them *do* know somebody — or are somebody themselves.

The following people are especially likely to have writing and/or publishing contacts:

Anyone living in or near New York, Los Angeles, or Toronto

Anyone with a good deal of money

Any upper-class or upper-middle-class professional (a doctor, lawyer, middle manager, college teacher or administrator, etc.)

Anyone who is famous or well known in *any* field

It is fair game to ask anyone you know — politely, of course — if he or she can help you, or if he or she knows anyone who might be able to help you. For example, if you play racketball with the brother of a fiction editor at *Redbook*, ask him to give his sister a call, and to mention that you're an acquaintance of his and will be sending her a short story soon. Send this story promptly, and begin your cover letter with something like this: "Your brother Martin suggested that I show you this story, 'To the Smokehouse.' I believe he mentioned me and my work to you when you spoke with him earlier this week."

Sometimes one contact will lead to another in a chain — for example, your sister's boss may know an editor's secretary. That's fine so long as it leads you, however circuitously, to the right person. Christina Baldwin sold her book *One to One* in such a manner. When she learned of a conference on women in writing, she wrote the director and told her of her unpublished book, and of her work teaching. She was invited to be a panelist at the conference. At the conference she was introduced to agent Meredith Bernstein. Baldwin gave Bernstein her manuscript. Bernstein liked it, agreed to represent it, and took it to an editor at Evans and Company. Ten days later, Bernstein had made a deal with Evans.

Most writers, of course, aren't as fortunate as Baldwin. Sometimes a chain of contacts will lead nowhere, or in circles.

When this happens, just shrug it off and pursue other potential contacts.

Does where you live have a bearing on the kind and number of useful contacts you're likely to have or make? Of course it does, and so do many other factors. If you are a well-to-do white-collar professional living in or near New York, many of the people you know probably have publishing contacts, or are involved in publishing themselves. But if you are a janitor in Billings, Montana, you are of course not going to have as easy a time making helpful contacts. Nevertheless, you may be surprised at how much you can do in Billings.

Making contacts boils down to nothing more or less than getting to know people through letters, phone calls, and face-to-face meetings. It's largely a matter of being friendly, willing to approach people, able to listen well, and able to hold a pleasant conversation. It requires one part sociability, one part savvy, and one part chutzpah.

There are probably as many ways of making contacts as there are people who can be helpful to you. Here, however, are some strategies that have worked for many writers in the past:

- Use available resources. If you want to get to know some other writers of children's books in your area, call the Society of Children's Book Writers and ask for some names and addresses. Use library reference books (*Contemporary Authors, Something About the Author, The Writers Directory*, etc.) to locate writers directly.

- Talk with bookstore owners and managers, librarians, and creative writing teachers at colleges and universities. Most will be happy to spend a few minutes with you and share what they know. Appointments usually aren't necessary, though college teachers keep very limited office hours, so it is a good idea to find out what these are in advance by calling the department office.

- Don't be afraid to call up a stranger to ask for advice or information. Most people are gracious and willing to help. But don't take up too much of a person's time. I'm usually happy to speak with anyone for about fifteen minutes; beyond that, however, I begin to feel put-upon.

• Attend readings by published fiction writers, writers' conferences, and other writers' gatherings. Don't be afraid to approach people to talk and ask questions. A list of writers' conferences throughout North America appears every May in *Writer's Digest*.

• Join your local writers' center or writers' club.

• Join a professional writers' organization, e.g., The Authors Guild. If you're a genre writer, join the organization for professional writers in your genre. Offer to be of service to the organization, by serving on a committee or doing gruntwork (typing, envelope stuffing, etc.).

• Join the National Writers Union and/or the National Writers Club.

• Take a writing class taught by a well-published fiction writer.

• If there's someone you'd like to talk with, preferably alone, for a few minutes, invite him or her to breakfast or lunch at a good restaurant. This is a very effective inducement, since most people enjoy good food, and since it doesn't take up much of the person's time—after all, he or she has to eat anyway. You should, of course, pick up the tab (it's 80 percent tax deductible) and leave a reasonable tip (also 80 percent deductible).

• A contact can only become useful if you ask questions, so ask for what you need: "Can you recommend an agent who's good at selling science fiction novels?" "What's the name of one of the fiction editors at *The New Yorker*?" "What do you know about Algonquin Books?"

Never lose sight of the purpose of all this: to interest editors, book packagers, or agents in your work; to get that work into their hands; and to build your writing career.

ETIQUETTE FOR MAKING AND USING CONTACTS

There are clear rules of etiquette for making and dealing with contacts. In general, these follow the basic rules of common sense and compassion. For example, don't be obnoxious or demanding; don't ask for more than someone is able or willing to provide; and don't keep pushing if your request for help is denied. Here are some more specific guidelines:

● When you first write, call, or meet someone whose name you have been given by a mutual contact, mention the name of that contact almost immediately. For example, you might begin a phone conversation this way: "Hi, Marilyn. My name is Scott Edelstein; I believe Helen McIntosh spoke with you last week about my work." A letter might begin: "Dear Nancy: George Jarvis suggested that I send you the enclosed novel proposal, *A Farewell to Ohms*. George is a fan of the book, and he tells me that he recommended it to you a few days ago."

● When following up an earlier letter, phone call, or meeting, refer to it at the beginning of your letter or conversation. For example, a letter might begin: "Dear Irving: I enjoyed meeting and talking with you at the North Woods Writers' Conference last month. I'm glad you're interested in looking at some of my short stories, and I'm enclosing my most recent piece, 'Ohio Lust.'" This clearly establishes your connection and reminds the person of what he or she promised to do for you.

● The less time, energy, or effort it takes to respond to your request, the more likely it is to be granted. If you ask a well-known writer, "What's the name of your editor at Dutton?" you'll probably be given the editor's name. But if you ask, "Would you read my novel?" the answer will usually be no. Your chances of getting someone to read a six-page story are usually about 50 percent.

● Don't grovel, whine, plead, lie, falsely flatter, or bribe anyone. These are sleazy, and they rarely work.

● Remain friendly and polite at all times. If for some reason the other person doesn't act this way to you, end the conversation or correspondence.

• Be aware of the other person's time, needs, and other commitments. Don't overstay a welcome, monopolize or overextend a conversation, or make the person late for another appointment.

• Always ask; never demand.

• If you are trying to reach someone by phone but can only get through to a secretary, spouse, boyfriend, etc., leave a message that includes your name, phone number, and reason for calling. For long distance calls, it is a good idea to add, "Calling collect is fine." If your call is not returned after three business days, try again. After three unsuccessful tries, take the hint and give up.

• If someone agrees to help you at a future date but doesn't, repeat your request after a few weeks. Repeat it again a few weeks later if necessary. If after three requests the person still hasn't fulfilled a promise, he or she probably never will. Don't berate this person; simply give up.

• When asking another writer for assistance, offer your own help in exchange (if you have help you can give). Usually this will be information or referrals—the name of a contact of your own, information about a publication you write for, etc.

• When someone assists you, express thanks. If your contact expends some significant time and effort in the process, send a short, polite thank-you note or card. If someone makes a genuinely major effort on your behalf, a small gift is appropriate.

• If someone says no to your request, accept that answer gracefully. But if someone postpones helping you, take that postponement at face value. For instance, if someone says, "Call me again about this in April," do just that.

• Once you are in a position to help make contacts for other talented writers, do so unstintingly on request.

CHECKLIST

Useful contacts:
- Editors
- Agents
- Other publishing employees (marketing people, sales representatives, editors' secretaries, etc.)
- Other writers
- Writing teachers
- Bookstore owners and managers
- Librarians
- Staff people at writers' centers and writers' organizations
- Famous and well-known people in any field
- Wealthy and well-to-do people, particularly professionals
- Anyone living in or near New York, Los Angeles, or Toronto
- Anyone you know who knows people in publishing

CHAPTER 9

NOVEL PROPOSALS: WHAT THEY ARE, HOW THEY WORK, AND WHEN TO USE THEM

AS YOU KNOW BY NOW, it is sometimes possible to sign a contract with a publishing company to publish your novel before you've even written most of it. What makes this possible is a sales tool called a novel proposal: a carefully assembled package that clearly outlines the book and, equally clearly, demonstrates that you've got the ideas and talent to complete it.

Each novel proposal includes at least one sample chapter (more often three or more), a plot synopsis for most or all of the book (usually called an *outline*), an author biography, and optional supporting materials such as endorsements, reviews, and/or samples of your published fiction. A proposal is sometimes called a *portion and outline*, even though it usually includes other items as well. Chapters 11 and 12 provide complete step-by-step instructions for preparing a proposal for your novel; this chapter will explain how to use a proposal, and when using one is most appropriate.

Proposals offer advantages to both writers and publishers. A proposal enables a writer to secure a contract (and, typically, part of an advance) from a publisher without first having to compose the entire book. This usually means not only some money up front, but a near-guarantee of an additional sum once the book is completed to the publisher's satisfaction. And if no publisher is interested in the proposal, the writer doesn't have to finish the book at all.

For a publisher, signing a contract with a writer based on a proposal means that the writer is committed to completing the book by a certain date. This enables the publisher to plan for and schedule the publication and promotion of the book well in advance.

But some of these advantages are drawbacks at the same time. If you sign a contract for your novel based on a proposal, you'll be expected to complete the book by your deadline—or forfeit whatever money you've received for the project so far. It also means you must generally adhere to the plot in your novel outline. In short, you've made a commitment that you'll be expected to live up to.

Furthermore, even though you may sign a contract with a publisher based on your proposal, that publisher is never obligated to publish the finished book. Certainly it hopes and plans to do so; but your contract will allow your publisher to cancel the deal if it is unhappy with the completed novel. You may also be required to return any advance money you've received.

Not every book lends itself to the proposal format. Try to imagine, if you can, a plot synopsis for *Catch-22*, *Moby Dick*, or *Finnegans Wake*. If your own novel can't be well represented by a few sample chapters and a plot synopsis, don't attempt a proposal. Finish the book before you put it on the market.

Many novels *can* be well represented in proposals, however—particularly genre novels and novels with strong, clear plots. If you have solid finished drafts of a few of your chapters (ideally the initial ones), and can come up with a cohesive, intriguing outline of the rest, you may have a salable proposal on your hands.

Should you try to sell your novel on the basis of a proposal? This depends on many different factors, which I'll examine one by one.

First, it should go without saying that any proposal must be engaging or entertaining. If it isn't, don't try to sell it, because you don't have something worth selling. Either the proposal needs work or the whole novel does.

If you're a lazy or undisciplined writer, or write quite slowly, or can find very little time to write, then offering publishers a proposal, no matter how well done it may be, is not a very good idea. You'll have to finish the book by an agreed-upon deadline, and unless you have enough time, energy, and discipline, you're not going to meet that deadline.

Let's assume, however, that you're able to write a strong, interesting proposal for the novel you're working on; that you'll be able to meet a reasonable deadline for finishing the book; and that the completed book will adhere reasonably closely to your plot synopsis. Should you go ahead and offer publishers a proposal, or should you finish the whole book first?

Much depends on your own track record as a writer. If you can show that you are a reliable, experienced professional, an editor should have few qualms about making a commitment based on a proposal; but if you've published little or nothing before, the editor will probably feel very uneasy about signing a contract with you based on anything less than a complete manuscript. And even if the editor wants to buy your proposal, the other folks at the publishing house (the publisher, the marketing people, etc.) may tie his or her hands.

The best way to convince an editor that you're a trustworthy pro is to have already sold or published a novel, preferably with a major publisher. While it would be nice if this novel were still in print and selling well, it isn't essential; what's important is that your editor has concrete evidence that you can write a complete, publishable novel.

If you haven't sold a novel already, other *significant* credentials can often be helpful, though usually less so than a previous novel sale. For example, if you've published at least one book-length work of nonfiction (again, preferably with a major press), this tells editors that you know how to put a publishable full-length book together. (If your nonfiction book is a single extended narrative, written much as a novel would be but with an entirely factual "plot," this will be particularly helpful.) Or if you've published a dozen short stories and a couple of novellas in reputable magazines, these tell editors that you're an experienced and well-published fiction writer capable of working in longer lengths. Either of these sets of credentials *may* be enough to make editors feel fairly comfortable about buying a proposal from you.

If you have a proposal for a genre novel, having sold or published several stories *in that same genre* can be as helpful, or nearly as helpful, as a novel sale. These publications show editors not only that you're a pro, but that you're familiar with the field. If one of these stories has become part of your proposed novel, or has evolved into that novel, that's better still: it means that part of the novel has already passed the test of publication. It was both these circumstances that helped Ron Cross sell his first novel, *Prisoners of Paradise*, to Franklin Watts, on the basis of a proposal.

If you've got no or very few significant fiction sales or publications, forget about selling your novel via a proposal. You won't be able to. Finish your novel before you try to market it.

The type of novel you want to publish also has a strong bearing on whether you should go the proposal route. With few exceptions, genre novels are *much* easier to sell via proposals than adult mainstream novels. Mainstream novels and novellas for younger readers are somewhat easier to sell via proposals than mainstream adult novels; but they are still tougher to sell than genre books. (Books shorter than novella length are so short that they cannot be sold via proposals.)

What if your shorter publications are in one genre but you want to sell a novel in another? In general, you'll need to finish your novel before you try to sell it. Romance editors aren't going to be impressed by your publications in science fiction magazines. Exceptions to this rule: horror, fantasy, and science fiction are considered related genres: publications in any of the three genres will impress editors in the other two.

The situation is less clear-cut when you've written a proposal for one age group and most or all of your previous sales and publications are in another. These two rules apply, however: 1) the narrower the gap in age, the more your credentials will mean; and 2) your proposal can be for a younger age group than your shorter work, but not an older one. If you've published a fair amount of adult short fiction, these publications will help you sell your novel proposal for young adults. But if your publications have been mostly for children and young adults, don't expect to be able to sell your first adult novel on the basis of a proposal.

The question of genre can sometimes outweigh that of age, however. If you've published nine or ten mystery stories for adults and want to sell your proposal for a mystery novel for middle readers (ages 8-12), you've got a decent shot at selling the proposal because of your strong genre credentials.

Remember, too, that having published a novel for a readership of *any* age is always a huge plus. Even if your one previously published novel was a western for young readers, and your proposal is for an adult fantasy or mainstream novel, the publication of your western tells editors that you're a professional capable of turning out a complete, publishable novel.

One other factor can make a big difference in how editors respond to your proposal, and that's the amount of text you include. The larger the portion of your book that you provide, the more material the editor has to judge, and the less risky saying yes becomes. Therefore, the smaller the number of previous publications and other credentials that you have, the larger a portion of the entire book you should include. If you're proposing a 60,000-word young adult novel and your previous publications are limited to seven short stories in three mid-size literary magazines, you would be wise to include at least 30,000 words of sample chapters and a very thorough outline of the remainder. But if you've already published one or two westerns and want to sell another, forty pages of sample chapters (or simply one long chapter) and a good six-page outline will probably be sufficient.

The anticipated length of your book also makes a difference: the longer the length, the more material you'll need to provide. (I should add that, in general, editors are very hesitant to buy proposals for novels of over 100,000 words from writers who have not already sold at least one other book; in fact, because of the higher publication costs and potentially higher financial risk, editors are a bit hesitant even to buy completed novels over 100,000 words.)

What if you include, say, three sample chapters in your proposal, and the editor or one or more other people at the press feels they're not enough? It's unlikely that the editor will simply return the proposal to you. It is equally unlikely, however, that he or she will come up with a contract. The editor will almost always ask to see more, probably another one to three chapters, perhaps as much as the remainder of the novel, before making a decision. This leaves you with three choices: write and submit the additional chapters; ask for the proposal back and hope that another editor will buy the proposal as is; or insist that the editor make a final decision based on what you've submitted so far. If you take this third option, 95 percent of the time the answer will be a regretful no. You can also, of course, choose to write some but not all of the new material the editor has requested; sometimes this will do the trick.

A great many editors regularly read proposals and offer publishing contracts based on them. Some even prefer proposals to finished manuscripts. Some other editors, however, never (or almost never) buy proposals at all, only completed books. A few publishing houses even have an outright policy against buying novels (or, in one case I know of, first novels) on the basis of proposals. It's possible, then, that an editor may like your proposal very much, but return it with a note saying, "Show this to me again once it's finished," or "If the finished book turns out this well, I'd love to publish it." While this always indicates genuine interest, the editor is committed to nothing.

Some other points regarding novel proposals:

• When a publishing house offers you a contract to publish your book based on your proposal, it will almost certainly offer you an advance. The amount of this advance is usually negotiable. Normally advances are paid in two parts: half on or shortly after the signing of the contract, and half on or shortly after acceptance of the finished manuscript. If you are not offered this half-and-half arrangement, ask for it—and push hard for it if necessary.

• Your publishing contract will be contingent on your turning in an acceptable final manuscript. If the publishing firm decides that your finished novel isn't acceptable for any reason, it has the right to either request a rewrite or cancel your contract. If the contract is cancelled, you get back all rights to your book, but you don't get the rest of your advance—and the publisher may also demand that you return some or all of the advance money you've already received.

● If a publishing house accepts your book proposal and offers you a contract but no advance, press for one. Without the payment of an advance, the publisher can decide at any time and for any reason not to publish your book; there will be nothing you can do about it, and you won't have received a penny for your efforts.

CHECKLIST

You may offer publishers a novel proposal in lieu of a completed book if:
- Your novel can be condensed into a strong, engaging plot synopsis.
- You are capable of working under and meeting a reasonable deadline.
- You can show through prior sales and/or publications that you are a reliable professional who is able to turn out a good novel. Normally this means having sold a previous novel to a major publisher, but in certain cases having sold short fiction and/or book-length nonfiction will suffice.
- You can include as sample material a major portion of the book, preferably the first few chapters. The less significant your previous sales and publications are, the more sample material you should provide.

PART II
USEFUL TOOLS

CHAPTER 10

WRITING SUCCESSFUL COVER AND QUERY LETTERS

First, a review of some definitions:

A *cover letter* (sometimes called a *covering letter*) is a brief—usually not more than one page—letter accompanying and introducing a manuscript. A cover letter may also, when appropriate, introduce yourself and/or your publications and credentials. Use a cover letter whenever you send a manuscript to an editor, agent, book packager, or other publishing professional.

A *query letter* (sometimes simply called a *query*) should be used only when you are not permitted to submit an unsolicited manuscript. Queries are similar to cover letters in tone, but they describe a manuscript in much more detail, and they serve a very different purpose: to interest the recipient in that manuscript and get him or her to ask to see it. With few exceptions, the only query letters you will have to write are initial letters to agents.

COVER LETTERS

Suppose you have a short story that you wish to publish. You could simply slip it in an envelope, along with a return envelope and return postage, and mail it off to editors. But to many editors that would be both impersonal and amateurish. After all, you are not merely a writing machine sending a product to an editing machine; you are a human being making contact with another human being. A cover letter establishes a person-to-person relationship, however tenuous, between you and the recipient of your manuscript.

But there is a much more important purpose to a cover letter. It is a way to let people know of your previous publications, other credentials, and appropriate background. It is your chance to quickly establish yourself as a professional, and as a writer worth reading—before your recipient has read a word of your manuscript.

Use a tone that is businesslike but friendly. Be clear and concise. Remember that a cover letter is not an overt sales pitch. Don't tell your reader what a genius you are or how stupendous your work is. Don't plead, wheedle, grovel or ask for criticism, either. Simply cite your writing credentials and any background directly relevant to your piece.

Your cover letter should not include a synopsis or detailed description of your manuscript. You may, however, provide a few words of description, e.g., "a fantasy story set in medieval times," "a family saga with a Spanish setting," "a traditional murder mystery," etc.

An example of a good cover letter appears on page 123. This letter is meant to accompany the submission of an unsolicited short story to a hypothetical literary magazine called *Great Plains Review*. In four brief paragraphs, this letter demonstrates that its author is a serious and productive writer; that she is a published professional with relevant academic credentials; that she has had special experience that informs her story; and that she is a regular and appreciative reader of the magazine.

Writing a good cover letter means presenting your credentials and background in the most positive way you can. In her letter to Todd Kraft, Helen Gould lists four literary magazines in which her work appeared, but she doesn't mention that all four pieces were short poems. As for her M.A., she has been enrolled in the program only three weeks. Nevertheless, what she says is true and accurate.

When presenting your credentials, omit anything trivial or marginal, such as publication of a short story in your church newsletter, or Honorable Mention in the Toledo Writers' Guild's 1988 short fiction competition.

4102 Hennepin Ave.
Minneapolis, MN 55410
(612) 555-9098

March 19, 1990

Mr. Todd Kraft
Editor, <u>Great Plains Review</u>
3007 LaSalle
Milwaukee, WI 53211

Dear Todd Kraft:

I wanted you to have a chance to see my newest story, "Breakfast at Midnight," which I'm enclosing, along with a return envelope and return postage.

The story is set in Grenada during the American military invasion in 1984. I was in Grenada at the time as a tourist; though this piece is fiction, some of the details and events are taken from my own experience during the first hours of the invasion.

My previous work has appeared in several publications, including <u>Milkweed Chronicle</u>, <u>Great River Review</u>, <u>Loonfeather</u>, and <u>The Lake Street Review</u>. My nonfiction (including two pieces on Grenada) has appeared in the <u>St. Paul Pioneer Press</u>. I've been writing for several years and am currently at work on my M.A. in creative writing at the University of Minnesota.

I've been reading and enjoying <u>Great Plains Review</u> since 1985, and always look forward to the next issue.

Sincerely,

Helen Gould

If you have no significant writing credentials at all, and no special background appropriate to the piece you're submitting, your cover letter will be simpler than Helen Gould's. It should be brief and to the point, and should resemble the example on page 125.

If your manuscript has been solicited—that is, if your recipient has asked to see it—your first paragraph will be somewhat different from those in the two sample letters. For example:

> Thank you for your letter of December 9. As you requested, I'm sending along a copy of my novel, *Cat's Pajamas*.

If you have previously described your publications, background, and experience in a query letter to the same person, you need not fully reiterate them in your cover letter. It is not a bad idea, however, to touch on your major publications again briefly, and/or to mention again any background relevant to the specific manuscript. For example:

> You'll recall that I've published one previous novel with Dell Books, *Wichita Shuffle*, and that this new book is based largely on my experience as a guard in a minimum-security prison for white-collar criminals in Florida.

Don't overestimate the power of a cover letter. At best, it will help generate some initial interest in your manuscript. The best cover letter in the world won't make up for a manuscript that is poorly constructed, ill-conceived, or badly written. Ultimately, your work will stand or fall on its own merits.

QUERY LETTERS

The most important rule regarding query letters is this: don't use them unless you have to. If an editor or book packager reads unsolicited manuscripts, forget about querying. You already know that your work will be read, so send it.

90 Clemens Walk, Apt. 6
Orion, CA 94551
(415) 555-6774

June 4, 1990

Madeleine Baum
Fiction Editor, <u>Western Woman</u>
90822 Wilshire Blvd.
Los Angeles, CA 90009

Dear Ms. Baum:

    I felt you'd enjoy the enclosed short story, "Post Haste," and
hope you'll want to include it in a future issue of <u>Western Woman</u>.
Along with the piece I'm enclosing a return envelope and return
postage.

    I've been enjoying <u>Western Woman</u>--particularly its short
stories--for some time, and look forward to reading future issues.

    Please write or call if you have any questions.

                Sincerely,

                Cynthia Sternlicht

In practice, the only people a fiction writer will probably need to query are literary agents. Very few agents will look at an unsolicited manuscript, unless it is accompanied or preceded by a recommendation or referral from a mutual contact.

A good query introduces your manuscript (and, as appropriate, yourself and your credentials), puts the most positive spin on your work, and intrigues the recipient enough to ask to see your manuscript—that is, to solicit it.

. Most of your query letter should be devoted to describing and synopsizing your project. Although your query letter should be concise and to the point, you should provide enough description and detail to give the agent a clear sense of the book's plot, structure, and most important characters. To do this your letter will probably need to run at least one full single-spaced page, and possibly as many as two, which should be considered the maximum.

The first few sentences of your query letter should clearly and concisely let the agent know the following:

- Your significant publications and other writing credentials (awards, fellowships, editorial positions, etc.)
- The title and type of book (e.g., young adult, romance, adult mainstream, etc.) you wish to send
- Whether the project is in completed or proposal form
- The name of the person who recommended or referred you to the agent (if such a recommendation or referral was provided)

Once you've let the agent know these basics, you should plunge into the description of your project. How you write this description depends on the project itself. If you have a genre novel, for example, or a mainstream novel that is strongly plot-oriented, your description should be a clear, concise, highly condensed plot synopsis, very much like a novel outline (though briefer). Use the third person present tense, and stick closely to what happens as the plot unfolds, step by step.

If you have a somewhat quirkier book, your description can and should be equally quirky. Although you shouldn't avoid discussing the plot, you may also deal with characters, situation, and style in some detail. But don't simply talk *about* your style (e.g., "The novel will be written in a terse, humorous way."). Instead, *use* that style in your description. For example:

> The novel focuses on Margaret Blau, who, at the age of five, wanted to be a surgeon. Now, however, holding a scalpel above her sister's abdomen, she wishes she were five years old again. Somewhere in between she'd taken her medical boards and a husband. All she'd really wanted was a white outfit and plenty of bright light. "I should have become a Hindu," she thinks, "or a dentist."

Once you've finished this description of your project (which should run between half a page and 1½ pages), you're near the end of your letter. In your next paragraph, mention any background or experience, if any, that directly relates to your project—for instance, if you've written a novel about life in a Moscow orphanage and you spent a year in a Russian orphanage yourself.

Your final paragraph should ask the agent if he or she is interested in looking at your manuscript. Enclose a stamped, self-addressed business envelope for the agent's reply.

A sample query letter to an agent appears on pages 128-129. This is the actual letter mystery/suspense writer Mary Kuhfeld (who writes under the name Mary Monica Pulver) used to approach agents a few years ago. As a result of this letter, she became the client of a good agent, who has since sold not only *Murder at the War* but two of her other novels. *Murder at the War* was published by St. Martin's Press. In the example, the agent to whom the letter is addressed is imaginary.

Some acceptable variations on query letters:

• If you prefer, you may type up your project description separately. It should be 1½ or double-spaced, and should not exceed 8 pages (3-5 pages is best). Your query letter should be brief—no longer than a page and, ideally, less—and should refer the agent to the attached description.

• If you have more than one project that you wish to sell,

7307 W. Franklin Ave.
St. Louis Park, MN 55426
612-541-9827

August 19, 1984

Ms. Irma Genary
Author's Representative
8550 Lexington Ave.
New York, NY 10019

Dear Ms. Genary:

I am a mystery writer who has sold five stories to <u>Hitchcock's
Mystery Magazine</u> in the past eighteen months. The first of these
stories appeared in the March 1983 issue; the last is not yet in
print.

Two of the stories involve the hero of a murder mystery I have
written entitled MURDER AT THE WAR. The novel is traditional in
structure and set in an "exotic locale"--a simulated medieval war.
Every year 3000-plus members of the Society for the Advancement of
Medievalism gather at a campground in western Pennsylvania to hold
a mock war. Everyone dresses in medieval garb (including steel
armor for the fighters), and the campground joyously drops out of
the twentieth century for a three-day weekend. During the course
of a mock battle in the woods, however, a man is found dead--really
dead, not mock dead. The woman who finds him becomes the chief
suspect. She also happens to be the wife of Peter Brichter, a
police detective from out of state.

The local law enforcement officers are startled at the sight of all
these oddly dressed people and half-convinced they are some kind
of cult. Brichter, trying to clear his wife, begins his own
unofficial investigation, but the local police angrily call a halt
to his activities and confine him to his encampment.

Meanwhile, the clues lead to a certain Lord Christopher, who,
dressed in armor, participated in a mock skirmish beside the victim
shortly before the murder. Lord Christopher's armor is found
abandoned in the woods near the body, and it seems that no one had
seen or heard of him before he appeared in the woods, dressed for
battle.

All of this suggests that there is, in fact, no Lord Christopher
--that he was a SAM member who assumed that persona (and armor) as
a disguise only for a few minutes, for the specific purpose of
killing his victim and then escaping detection. There were two
hundred participants in the woods battle; any one of them might
have slipped away for a brief time.

While the local police struggle with the esoterica of the Society,
Brichter welcomes visitors in his tent, fitting the pieces together

Ms. Irma Genary
Page Two

in classic detective style.

There really is a medievalist society which holds an annual mock
war in Pennsylvania. I am a member, and drew on my experiences at
several of these wars in writing this book.

The novel is in finished form, about 90,000 words long. Please let
me know if you would be interested in reading it with an eye toward
representing it.

Sincerely,

Mary Kuhfeld

you may discuss as many as two of them in a query letter. If you have more than two, mention only the two best or most salable ones. If you become that agent's client, you can bring up other projects later. If you do discuss two different projects, your query should still not exceed two pages; if you attach separate plot synopses, try to make them no longer than five pages each.

● If your project lends itself well to a brief (one to three-minute) verbal description, *and* you're a good speaker and conversationalist, you may wish to telephone agents instead of writing query letters. Most agents don't object to telephone queries; those that do will simply ask you to put your query in writing. This is a legitimate request, not a put-off. The more previous publications or sales you have, the more receptive an agent is likely to be to a telephone query.

Once an agent agrees to look at your work, don't just dump it in an envelope and mail it. Remember to include a brief cover letter, thanking the agent for his or her interest and referring to both the enclosed manuscript and the letter or phone call in which the agent requested a look at it. Remember to enclose a return envelope and return postage.

QUERYING EDITORS AND BOOK PACKAGERS

If an unsolicited submission to an editor or book packager is returned unread, along with a note insisting that you query first, you should follow the above guidelines for writing a query, with one obvious exception: the final paragraph should not discuss possible representation. To transform the query letter on pages 128-129 from a query directed toward agents into one directed toward editors and book packagers, simply remove the last six words of the final paragraph.

It is *extremely* unlikely that you will ever have a short story manuscript returned unread with a note telling you that you must query first. If this does happen to you, however, don't waste your time and postage; your chances of selling to this market are virtually zero. If you do wish to query nevertheless, use the same basic approach of first identifying your publications and other credentials, then synopsizing your plot. Keep your letter no longer than one full page, however.

CHECKLISTS

A successful cover letter:

- Establishes a person-to-person contact between you and your recipient.
- Presents your publications and other credentials as a writer as positively as possible.
- Is no more than one page long.
- Lists any background or experience that is relevant to your submission.
- If appropriate, refers to a previous phone call or letter, or to a recommendation or reference from a mutual contact.
- Gives a good first impression of you and your work.
- Is not an overt sales pitch or a piece of self-promotion.
- Cannot work miracles.

A successful query letter:

- Is no more than two pages long.
- Is primarily devoted to describing and synopsizing your project, and does so clearly, intriguingly, and positively. Use a style and approach similar to that of the project itself.
- Clearly indicates whether the project is in finished or proposal form.
- Lists your publications and other writing credentials in as positive a manner as possible.
- Explains any background or experience you may have that relates to the project.
- If appropriate, refers to a recommendation or referral from a mutual contact.
- Asks whether the recipient would like to see the project.
- Is accompanied by a #10 stamped return envelope.
- Evokes a positive response.

CHAPTER 11

THE ART OF WRITING THE NOVEL OUTLINE

NOVEL OUTLINES HAVE NOTHING TO DO with the formal outlines you may have written in school. In fact, they're not outlines as we generally think of them at all. A much more accurate term would be *plot synopses*; in book publishing, however, the term *outline* has the same meaning, and is much more frequently used.

A novel outline is a narrative synopsis of your book's plot. Put another way, it is a heavily condensed version of your book. The emphasis should not be on themes or settings or characters, but on plot, on what happens. Of course you will be revealing character, atmosphere, motivation, and setting as the outline proceeds; but all of this must be done through your plot, and must be subordinate to it. It should go without saying that your outline should be clear, concise, and engaging.

Novel outlines are usually written in the third person present. The first person present is acceptable *if* your novel has a first-person narrator and the first person yields a clear, interesting outline. Jack Bickham's outline for *Tiebreaker*, which begins on page 151, is written in the first person present. Never use the past tense in a novel outline except in occasional passages.

The beginning and ending of your outline should read and feel like a beginning and ending, even in their heavily condensed form.

The trick to writing a good outline is to focus on events occurring moment by moment, as if the reader (and you, the writer) were there watching them happen. Here, for example, is a scene or chapter as it might appear in a novel outline:

Darla drives away, furious, and swears that she will never talk to her father again. Knowing that now she won't be able to sleep, she drives to the cemetery where her mother is buried, parks, and climbs over the fence. She manages to slip past the guard and struggles in her high heels through the snow in search of her mother's grave. There is no moon, and she cannot find the grave amid the snowdrifts and darkness. Finally she sits down against a tree, shivering, and cries for several minutes. Suddenly exhausted, she stands up and begins retracing her steps — and is arrested by the guard, who had followed her and watched her as she sobbed, huddled up in the snow.

Note that this narrative does *not* include explanatory asides, static descriptions, a statement of the author's intentions, or literary analysis of any kind. Such things are not merely unnecessary, but very much to be avoided in a novel outline; they get in the way. Here is precisely the sort of thing a novel outline must *not* contain:

In this scene, Darla comes face to face with her own anger and grief. The cemetery scene will be at once tense and touching, and in it Darla will realize for the first time how much her mother had meant to her.

The above paragraph doesn't show the reader anything at all; it merely explains things, laboriously and tediously. Instead of giving the reader events and experiences, it systematically snatches them away and replaces them with dull explanation and analysis. Your reader wants — and deserves — to be shown things as they happen, not merely to be told about them.

Most novel outlines are broken into chapters at the same spots where chapter breaks will probably occur in the finished novel. If, however, you feel that a single unbroken narrative will result in a better outline, you may choose this format instead. If you go the standard route and use chapter breaks, you may begin each new chapter on either the same or a new page, as you prefer.

Novel outlines should be typed according to standard manuscript form; see pages 45-58 for details.

If the sample chapters in your novel proposal are the first chapters in your book, you may begin your outline where the sample chapters leave off, or you may begin with Chapter One, synopsizing the sample chapters as well as the remainder of the book. Jack Bickham's outline for *Tiebreaker* (see page 151) takes the first route, beginning about 130 pages into the book, at the place where his sample chapters end.

If your sample chapters are not consecutive, or if Chapter One is not one of your sample chapters, then your outline *must* begin at the very beginning of the book.

Some novelists who provide consecutive sample chapters divide their outlines into two parts. The first part briefly synopsizes the action in the sample chapters; the second offers a far more detailed synopsis of the remainder of the book. Ronald Anthony Cross selected this format for the outline of his novel *Prisoners of Paradise* (see page 140). The first part of his outline reiterates the action in the forty pages of sample chapters included in the proposal.

If you like, you may include as the first page(s) of your outline a Cast of Characters section. This lists all the major and supporting characters by name and gives a one or two-sentence description of each person's background, circumstances, personality, and/or relationship to other characters. A sample Cast of Characters page appears on page 141.

How long should your outline be? It all depends on how complex your plot is, how long the book will run, how many sample chapters you have provided, and whether it synopsizes the entire book or only the portion not covered by the sample chapters. I've heard of outlines as short as four double-spaced pages and as long as eighty. Ten to fifteen pages is about average. Use whatever length you need to give a clear sense of the book's plot and pacing. When in doubt, it is usually better to err on the side of length; it's hard to explain a plot in too much detail, and very easy to be too brief. Remember, you are asking an editor to offer a contract and hard cash based on material he or she hasn't read yet; the clearer a picture you can give that editor of what your novel will be like, the more comfortable he or she will feel about agreeing to publish it.

Once you sell your novel on the basis of a proposal, do you have to adhere strictly to your outline? Not necessarily. Editors understand that novels often evolve as they are written, and thus they will usually go along with small and moderate changes. If you are contemplating any significant change of any kind, however — a different ending, the addition or deletion of a major character, a very different tone or setting, or a book that is much shorter or longer than originally contracted for — you should get in touch with your editor immediately to discuss the situation.

Two sample novel outlines appear in the Appendix. The first, *Prisoners of Paradise* by Ronald Anthony Cross, is for a science fiction novel which was published in 1988 by Franklin Watts. The second, *Tiebreaker* by Jack Bickham, is for an espionage novel involving the world of professional tennis, which was published by Tor Books in 1989.

CHECKLIST

A novel outline:
- Is a heavily condensed version of your entire novel.
- Must focus on plot.
- Should be written in the present tense.
- Should normally be in the third person (though first person is sometimes acceptable).
- Must be typed in standard manuscript format.
- May contain a Cast of Characters page, in which each character is briefly described.
- Need not be followed to the letter when you complete the novel.

CHAPTER 12

ASSEMBLING YOUR NOVEL PROPOSAL

A NOVEL PROPOSAL IS FIRST AND FOREMOST a selling tool. It is what you use to induce editors, marketing people, and other publishing folk to offer you a contract. When writing a proposal, then, you must do more than simply follow the proper format. You must create a proposal that is engrossing and rewarding on its own, *and* that promises a well-crafted, entertaining, and satisfying novel.

Your novel proposal should consist of at least these items:
- A proposal folder
- A cover page
- Your author biography
- One or more sample chapters (usually, the more the better)
- A narrative plot synopsis, usually called an outline

A cover letter should accompany all of this material, though it is not part of the propsal itself. You may also add to your proposal one or more of the following items:
- One or more endorsements, to a maximum of four, from well-known writers and/or other personalities.
- One or more published reviews of your earlier work. These may be of your shorter work, one or more previous books, or both. Excerpts from reviews are fine.
- Photocopies of your previously published work, from one to three pieces or excerpts, up to a maximum of twenty-five 8½-by-11-inch pages.

Let's assemble a proposal for your novel step by step. First, purchase a paper two-pocket 9-by-12-inch folder, the kind without a gusset (a strip used for binding in three-hole paper). It should be a dark or subdued color—brown, grey, dark blue, or black. Carefully remove the price tag.

Type the title of your novel, in all capital letters, on a blank stick-on label. Two lines beneath the title type your by-line, either real or pseudonymous (e.g., "by Ernestine Hemingway"). Stick this label in the exact center of the front cover of the folder. Type a second label with your name, address, and phone number(s). Attach this about four inches above or below the first label.

Prepare your cover page according to the guidelines on pages 53-54; see the example on page 48 for a visual guide.

Next prepare your author biography; follow the guidelines on pages 92-96; page 94 provides a visual guide. This biography belongs immediately after your cover page.

Your proposal must include at least one sample chapter—preferably more. (See page 117 for guidelines on how much sample material to provide.) This material should give readers a clear sense of the book's style, a good chunk of its plot, and a strong feel for at least one or two of its major characters. These chapters should be good, strong, solid pieces of writing that substantially advance your book's plot. The chapters should also, of course, be entertaining and engrossing in themselves. Place these chapters in the order in which they will appear in the finished book.

Normally your proposal should include the opening chapter(s) of your novel. It is sometimes acceptable to include one or more later chapters, either in addition to or in place of material from the beginning of the book. However, you may do so only if this later material gives readers a firm, clear sense of your characters, plot, and style.

If you are including more than one chapter, begin each chapter on a new page, following the format described on page 51 and illustrated on page 49.

The final item in your proposal will be your outline, which was discussed in detail in the previous chapter. If (and only if) you are not including your first chapter as a sample, your outline should *precede*, rather than follow, your sample chapter(s).

Now it's time to physically put the proposal together. In the right-hand pocket, all clipped together with a butterfly clamp, place the following items, in the following order (from top to bottom):

- Your cover letter, either flat or folded in thirds inside a #10 envelope, on which you have typed the recipient's name. (If you prefer, this letter or envelope may be paper-clipped to the outside front cover of the folder.)
- Your title page
- Your author biography
- One or more sample chapters
- The novel outline

If your proposal is unsolicited, or if you are sending it to an agent, you will need to enclose a return envelope or mailing bag and return postage (or International Reply Coupons).

If you are including any of the additional items discussed earlier in this chapter, place them in the left-hand pocket of the folder, behind the return postage. Either endorsements or reviews may go on top of the other pages, with samples of previously published work underneath. If you have a quote (either an endorsement or review) from a well-known writer, reviewer, or celebrity, this should definitely go on top, where it will be immediately visible to the recipient when he or she opens the proposal folder.

Place the proposal folder in a clasp envelope or mailing bag to which you have affixed typed mailing labels, including one for your return address. Weigh it, put sufficient postage on it, and ship it off. Then compliment yourself on a marketing job well done.

You know now that a successful writing career — however you may define that term — is the result of writing the best work you can and marketing it as intelligently and professionally as possible. This book has given you all the necessary tools; now it's up to you to provide the talent, the enthusiasm, and the pages full of words.

So roll up your sleeves and get started. Whether you're marketing your ninth novel, revising and researching markets for your new novella, or putting the opening paragraphs of your first short story on paper, I hope you'll make the best use of this book—and your own talent and skill—that you can. I'll be at my own typewriter, rooting for you.

CHECKLISTS

Your novel proposal *must* include:
- A 9-by-12-inch proposal folder
- A cover page
- Your author biography
- One or more sample chapters
- An outline
- An accompanying cover letter
- A return envelope and return postage (for unsolicited manuscripts and submissions to agents)

You *may* add one or more of the following items, as appropriate:
- Endorsements from well-known writers and/or personalities
- Published reviews of your work, or excerpts therefrom
- Photocopies of some of your previously published pieces, or excerpts thereof

Ronald Anthony Cross
1103 16th Street
Santa Monica, CA   90403
213/453-9508

Member, S.F.W.A.

PRISONERS OF PARADISE

by Ronald Anthony Cross

Background:

This is a novel of the far future. The scene is the Ultra
Ritz Luxury Vacation Resort Hotel. It's an enormous hotel
covering hundreds of square miles. The bottom floor consists of
a giant computer complex--the Hotel Mind. The hotel features
total environments (like Disneyland, only on a grander scale).
The Blue Lagoon Room, a tropical paradise, is an example.

Hard times: parts of the hotel have fallen into disrepair
and the guests, after hundreds of years of being cut off from the
outside, have degenerated into groups of warring savages.

On top of that, the computer has blocked off its awareness
of itself in its most advanced android bellboy (so that one part
of itself could experience freedom). That android immediately

Cross   Background/Characters/2

rebelled against the computer and now the hotel is at war with
itself.

The Characters

   Nightglider: Hotel explorer, loner, scout. A man deeply
versed in hotel lore, created in the spirit of those wild
untamable Indian scouts of the past. Chosen as prophet by the
Hotel Computer and the Adversary alike, his only desire is to be
free to explore unknown corridors.

   The Hotel Mind: The huge computer that covers the bottom
floor. Its one desire is to unite the dwellers in the hotel as a
work force to restore the hotel to its former glory.

   The Hotel Adversary: An android in a red bellboy outfit
with ornamental wings. A cunning creature waging a ceaseless war
against the Hotel Mind.

   Lana: A free-love, Blue Lagoon sex mate.

   Raindancer: A witch under the control of the Adversary
android, possessor of "power objects."

   Silky Death: A vicious little assassin, but a courageous
free spirit. A kinky chick.

PRISONERS OF PARADISE

by

Ronald Anthony Cross

<u>Chapters I - VII</u>

As you have seen from the portion, the first seven chapters serve to introduce Nightglider and establish his character as a lonely Hotel scout. They also introduce the Hotel Mind -- an enormous computer complex that covers the bottom floor of the Hotel -- and the Hotel Mind's chief adversary, a robot bell captain remote control that has turned against the Mind and is trying to take over the Hotel.

As the novel opens, Nightglider is in the process of leading a party of ruffians from the Shopping Center area who are searching for a secret entrance into the Tropical Lagoon Room, where all the brownskins live, with the hopes that they can break in and rob them. Nightglider knows there is no chance of this occurring, but nonetheless it's something the Shopping Center gang tries every so often.

Cross   2

He stashes them in a room, tells them to stay quiet, and
then goes to forage for food. After having a scrape with some
blind nightcrawlers (cannibals who have lost their vision from
generations of hiding in the dark, broken-down parts of the
Hotel), he returns with the food only to discover the Shopping
Center gang have grown restless and left the room. Worse, they
have been trapped and slaughtered by the brownskins. When
Nightglider goes to their rescue, he too is trapped and forced
into a fight to the death by the brownskins' most formidable
warrior, Big Knife. By using his wits he barely manages to kill
Big Knife, and almost gets killed himself in the process.

The brownskins take him back to the Lagoon Room, where they
have robots pull out his teeth in an initiation torture ceremony.
But a brownskin witch, Raindancer, who lives by herself and is a
follower of the Hotel Adversary (who gives her power objects in
exchange) is ordered by the Adversary to save Nightglider: he is
to play a key role in the war between the Adversary and the Hotel
Computer. Raindancer terrorizes the brownskins into adopting
Nightglider by operating a control which causes the Lagoon Room
to go into its Fourth of July celebration mode.

Cross   3

SUMMARY

Chapter VIII

N.G. comes to and finds himself with a new set of flashy
superplastic teeth. He is now in a semi-conscious ecstasy as
they have given him a strong painkiller. They rub him with the
Hotel supertan lotion (with a fast-acting stain to give you that
head start) and he spends a lot of recuperating time in sunrooms.
They also wheel him into the exercise room and he is strapped
down on a table and his muscles spasmed by electricity. A week
later and he is a brownskin with a flashy tan, perfect teeth, and
a more muscular build.

Chapter IX

There is a tribal celebration ceremony welcoming N.G. as a
blood brother, followed by a drunken party and a dance; after
this a game similar to musical chairs is played and he scores a
mate, the luscious Lana (named after the long-dead Hotel singer,
Lana Lomaine).

Cross   4

Chapter X

This chapter follows N.G. and Lana in their carefree
everyday lifestyle in the Tropical Lagoon Room. A mechanical
fish speaks to N.G. proclaiming him the chosen one, but N.G.
catches the fish and breaks it. Lana is stunned at his
sacrilege. They quarrel. Lana is both repulsed and confused by
his intense drive to freedom, but at the same time attracted by
his intensity--while N.G. has never experienced sex with such a
free sexy chick. He is strongly drawn to her. They make love.
Vow some kind of permanency.

Chapters XI & XII

Raindancer shows up and N.G. is forced to go with her.
She reveals to him that she is working for the Hotel
Adversary and has been given objects of power. She wants to
instruct him in the use of these power tools. But N.G. just
breaks them. N.G. is no good for anything but freedom.
Raindancer can't adjust to this. But now out of the conflict
between N.G. and Raindancer a new attraction-repulsion is born.
The two are extremely strong willed. Nightglider knows that she
draws her strength from her crazed dancing as he draws his from
running through dark corridors, from the solitude of uninhabited
realms. They make love. She tells him that her benefactor, the
android who gave her her power objects, has chosen N.G. as an
ally in his war against the Hotel Mind. N.G. is to go to the top
floor where the Adversary lives and be initiated into the service

of the android. (I decided to have the Devil in heaven and God
below for a change.)

To her amazement, he refuses. He doesn't want to help the
Hotel Computer or the Adversary. He also has decided he doesn't
want to stay in the Lagoon Room, paradise or no. He wants to
leave both women and run the corridors of the Hotel <u>alone</u>!
Besides, he adds, the piped-in music is driving him mad.

Raindancer communicates with the Adversary and later drugs
N.G. She implants a tracer bug in one of his plastic teeth,
under orders from the android.

<u>Chapter XIII</u>

We get out first view of the Adversary's kingdom on the top
floor, where he has gathered many of the Hotel's strangest
creations. The decor is of very weird and mixed themes. The
Adversary sends a giant robot to take N.G. prisoner.

N.G. awakens and finds out that the robot is after him and
can follow him because of the tracer bug Raindancer has placed on
him.

<u>Chapter XIV</u>

He breaks loose and runs for it. He breaks clear out of the
Lagoon Room and leads the robot off into the Hotel wilds. Nobody
can run like Nightglider; he even momentarily gets some distance
on the robot. His knowledge of the Hotel is awesome. He goes to
a floor frequented by thieves and assassins and other really hard

Cross   6

cases. He teams up with a tough little S&M chick, Silky Death,
who is a great assassin. He promises to sneak the chick and her
gang into the Lagoon Room so they can pillage it, if she'll help
him against the robot; weird sex follows!

Chapter XV

N.G. leads the robot into ambush but the robot destroys the
gang. This gives N.G. a good head start, though. He leads the
robot into unexplored territories. He replenishes himself in the
solitude he loves so well. He makes one last remarkable leap
across a chasm in the Hotel floor, hoping, of course, that he'll
make it and the robot will fall into the chasm. The robot,
however, pulls up short and applauds N.G.'s heroic leap. Just
then, Silky appears behind the robot, still alive but sorely
wounded: she has tracked them here. With her last strength she
throws herself on the robot, catapulting them both into the
chasm. N.G. is stunned by her courage. Once again he is free.

Chapter XVI

But not for long. Using a new tactic, the android pipes in
background music through the electronic bug that Raindancer had
planted on N.G. This horrid music follows him everywhere; he
gives in. He takes the elevator to the top floor. (The
elevators work, but the Hotel Mind has sealed off the bottom
floor, and the android has sealed off the top floor where he
hangs out.)

Chapter XVII

N.G. gets to the android. He is told by the android that
the Hotel Mind can block off the android from attacking it
because the android is only machinery, but that the android will
give N.G. great power in order to disable the computer.

He implants an electrode in N.G.'s head that gives him Hotel
Consciousness. His consciousness spreads out all over the Hotel
(this lends itself to some flashy descriptive prose). But N.G.
is not ready for Hotel Consciousness. He can't bear it.

Chapter XVIII

No way out, N.G. heads down to the basement to wreck the air
conditioner and sabotage the Hotel Computer. He overrides the
Hotel Mind when the computer tries to block off the elevator.

But when he gets down there, the computer tells him that it
is responsible for all Hotel life. If it's destroyed, Hotel life
will die, lights will go out, etc. It explains that it gave the
android the illusion of freedom by blocking out its awareness of
the computer deep inside itself, but that the android immediately
turned against the Mind. When N.G. asks why, the computer just
tells him that's the nature of things.

The computer now bargains with N.G. It will give him the
power to block out Hotel Consciousness or utilize it, at will.
He can block out the awful music whenever he wants. He can
activate the elevators and hold off the android or the computer
if they try to control him.

Due to his knowledge of the Hotel, the computer has made him

Cross   8

the chosen one. He is to unite his people at the Shopping Center
and the people of the Tropical Lagoon. Together they are to
start work on the holy task of repairing the Hotel. In several
generations it will be restored to all its glory.

N.G. agrees. The computer tells him that there is only one
forbidden fruit, that he is to promise not to ever visit Floor M.
N.G. promises and is transformed.

Chapter XIX

N.G. gets in the elevator and immediately presses "M,"
telling the Hotel Mind to fuck itself. He gets off at Mezzanine
and finally finds in the main gift shop some bottles of Purene
Mouthwash. Not knowing what mouthwash is, he drinks a bottle and
goes into a psychedelic state. Then he goes outdoors. Across
the street is another enormous hundred-square-mile resort hotel.

In between is an old man fishing for goldfish in a fountain.
They meet and exchange philosophies. "I never go indoors," the
old man tells N.G. But N.G. points out to him that everything is
indoors and that the sky is really a giant fake room like the
Blue Lagoon Room, only larger. The old man is convinced. He
leaves to start a new religion.

Chapter XX

N.G. returns to the Hotel and preaches his new religion, the
trinity. There are two giant hotels, the Ultra Ritz and another
one across the street. The two of them are contained within a
third, larger hotel, so enormous you can't see it. The sacrament

Cross

is to be Purene Mouthwash.

Chapter XXI

He unites the people, gets them stoned on Purene, but instead of repairing the Hotel they get together a giant war party to invade the hotel across the street.

N.G. is ecstatic. He realizes that he doesn't care about good and evil, or the religion he's using to control everyone, or the women he thought he loved (Lana, Raindancer, or Silky Death), or even his Hotel Consciousness: all he really cares about is exploring the corridors of the new hotel. It dawns on him that in some strange way he is the only really free being in the whole hotel. Or is he? He feels for an instant, deep down inside himself, some overwhelming but unnameable controlling force that is using him as a pawn--beyond Hotel! Beyond everything.

TIEBREAKER: the rest of the story in brief

Karyn Wechsting has found me in my room, regaining
consciousness, and is suspicious when I refuse to call the militia
or a doctor. I get rid of her and call the US embassy with a coded
message about a bridge game, which sets up a meeting. Fearing tiny
bugs in all my clothing and gear, I go out and buy some new locally
made sport clothes, and will wear them hereafter, taking other
security precautions as well. My meeting downtown with Mitchell,
from the embassy, is unsatisfactory; Nariv is missing. I am told
to rent a car and sit tight. Henry and Muriel Beamer, the American
tourists, appear in the hotel lobby and visit a bit.

On Sunday I visit the Lechova family, learn a lot more about
the conflicting currents in the family, and conduct a long taped
interview with Danisa in a park. Her motives for fleeing become
clearer and our mutual attraction grows. I am not aware of it at
the time, but Fjbk is watching us.

Maleeva's superior puts more pressure on him to find out more
about Smith. Altunyan, meanwhile, sends a coded message to Moscow,
asking for authority to do whatever is necessary to make sure
Danisa goes nowhere. In the United States, the CIA prepares false
ID papers and other "tourist" materials as part of its plot to get
Danisa out. A call comes in that they think they have spotted
Partek again, this time in Winnipeg.

On Monday, first round play begins with two-a-day matches.
Danisa and Hannah breeze through their first women's doubles match.
Fjbk threatens me directly about being too close to Danisa. A

contact delivers my phony ID materials to me, but it isn't clear
how I'm to use them. Ted Treacher is eliminated in the first round
of men's singles. Hannah wins her first singles match. I talk
with Danisa in the tunnel below the arena, and she hugs me. She
goes to the lockers, I start walking away, and an enraged Fjbk
comes out of the shadows. He kicks the shit out of me, says if I
touch her again he'll kill me, and leaves me leaking blood on the
pavement.

That night, I sit with Wechsting and Treacher and watch Danisa
win her first singles match. Afterward, the family learns she has
left the arena alone, which is totally unlike her.

It turns out that Danisa is by now in the back seat of a dirty
yellow VW belonging to the Beamers, who are headed out of Belgrade
with her, and plan to slip her across the border this very night.
They are the CIA's real plot. Danisa is left to assume that I
(Smith) have been deceiving her all along. But the Beamers run
into a routine traffic roadblock and have to turn back. Danisa
escapes after a harrowing car chase and heads home. The escape
attempt has been sunk.

At the same time, Sylvester closes in on Partek again in
Winnipeg, but Partek's new landlady inadvertently warns him and he
runs again, this time on a bus. Maleeva learns of the Beamer
intercept, and that Danisa is now back home. He does not connect
the two.

I am pleased Danisa is back home, but surprised and dismayed
when she is angry and bitter toward me. Since this meeting is at
her apartment, I can't talk to her. Her mother reveals to me that

she has seen through my cover, and is a potential ally because of the pressure always on Danisa from Leon Lechova.

On Tuesday morning a KGB contact man named Sislinsky flies into Belgrade and meets with Altunyan. Altunyan's idea of terminating Smith has been rejected. However, the KGB knows about the Beamers being stopped, and sees that they probably were trying to help Danisa. So Moscow has authorized Altunyan to do whatever is necessary to Danisa to make sure she can't leave.

At the same time, in Virginia, Dwight and Exerblein are called in by their CIA superior, who now knows that Partek has vanished again. He has also found a report from Belgrade about the Beamers' operation being aborted. This, it turns out, is the first a CIA higher-up has known about the whole operation. Dwight has been running slightly wild, mounting an Oliver North type operation largely on his own and filing routine reports that he knows probably won't be noticed in the storm of paper reports generated at Langley every day. Dwight's superior says they just can't mount an operation like this against a "friendly" and mostly non-aligned country, and says the whole thing is cancelled, and Smith is to be left twisting in the breeze.

That same morning, I put a flowerpot on my hotel balcony as a signal for a desired meeting to fill me in on what happened to Danisa last night. No one meets me, but I get a call from "Uncle Carl" in New York, saying all hope has been abandoned for the recovery of my sick Aunt Margaret. This is a signal to abort.

Fjbk shows up, wanting a truce with me. He is worried about Danisa's disappearance last night and says he will do anything to protect her. I say I know nothing.

Danisa wins her second match. Afterward, she won't speak to me. I am left puzzled, and Fjbk looks triumphant.

That evening, while Danisa is at the arena for her second match of the day, I go to a Reebok party and encounter Hannah and her mother. Hannah is cold, but Mrs. Lechova gets me aside and explains why she is for Danisa leaving the country: the pressure from Leon Lechova, the ever-watchful police, Fjbk's unhealthy interest. A pact forms between Mrs. Lechova and me. I will help if I can. She will bring Danisa to talk to me in the morning so the misunderstanding can be worked out. However, my code calls to the embassy, seeking a meeting to explain the abort signal, are not returned and I am on my own.

Wednesday morning we do meet. Danisa understands I didn't know anything about the Beamers and was not tricking her -- that instead I was being tricked, made a decoy without my knowledge. I am bitter about being set up, and intent on getting her out if I can figure a way.

Altunyan, meanwhile, is more convinced than ever that Smith is going to try to get Danisa out. He visits an agricultural shop, a druggist, and a doctor at a local hospital over whom he has some power.

In Queens, Dominic Partek reads about Danisa's exploits in the tourney so far, and finally concludes that he must go ahead and defect because she will always be a quasi-prisoner unless he is willing to go back to Russia and face probable execution. He makes a phone contact to an FBI man near the UN, and sets up a

meeting to turn himself in in Chappaqua the next evening.   A
secretary at the FBI office, however, blurts the information to a
lover, who in turn notifies a KGB spy.

By Wednesday afternoon, I make a desperation "Jack Black" call
to the embassy, which is the ultimate cry for a contact.   When it
is ignored, I go to the embassy in person and am told the operation
is off and Danisa is being abandoned.   Back at the arena with Karyn
Wechsting, I watch Danisa start her quarterfinal match against
Chris Evert.   It's a fine close match, but in game 7, Danisa
staggers and then collapses.

She is taken to a hospital where she is treated and put in
bed.   I see an aide scrubbing the handles of Danisa's rackets, and
figure out that something must have been painted on them to make
her sick.   I tell Fjbk this suspicion.   Danisa is weak but okay,
and will be released in the morning.

In New York, Sylvester drives toward Chappaqua, where he
intends to kill Partek.   Dwight and the FBI make plans for their
rendezvous with Partek and the taking of him into protective
custody.   In Belgrade, Fjbk encounters Altunyan in the parking lot
of the hospital after midnight and asks him what he knows about
Danisa's poisoning.   Altunyan, under pressure, says _he_ poisoned
Danisa with insecticide, but she's going to be okay and the illness
stopped her from trying to flee the country.   He mentions Fjbk's
old KGB links and swears him to secrecy and support.   Altunyan
hasn't counted on Fjbk's crazy love for Danisa, however, and Fjbk
goes nuts and strangles Altunyan on the spot, dumping his body in
a trash dumpster and running away.

When Danisa gets out of the hospital Thursday morning, I have a scheme set up. I give her details and she is weak and scared, but says okay. I have had a long talk with Karyn Wechsting and Ted Treacher late last night. I later call Danisa from the hotel room and ask her to come over for one more interview, and she says she will come right away.

Maleeva gets this report from his wiretap people, but Altunyan's body has been found and it's hitting the fan over that, and he is now pretty sure, as a result of seeing all of Smith's futile attempts at contacts with his superiors, that Smith's superiors have abandoned him. Therefore Maleeva keeps one man in the bug room next to Smith's hotel room, but pulls off other surveillance people to use them in the investigation of Altunyan's death.

Meanwhile, Hannah finds Danisa missing from home, and demands to know where she has gone, etc. Mrs. Lechova tells Hannah what has been going on -- including Smith's certainty that somebody poisoned Danisa's rackets. This puts Hanna squarely on the horns of a dilemma: the choice between love of family and loyalty to the state. She visits the shared bedroom, remembers a lot, makes her decision.

Maleeva checks by the bug room at the hotel and hears Smith and Danisa talking next door, a lengthy interview in progress. He awaits developments.

Using the car I rented earlier, I take Danisa to the airport. We are using Wechsting and Treacher's ID and passports. We fit the physical characteristics fairly well, and are wearing tinted glasses. We wait until the plane is almost ready to leave, and then try to rush through visa with other latecomers. Whether we would make it or not is problematical, but at that point there is a commotion nearby, and we see what anyone would think was Danisa, wearing her trademark blue, with her pigtail, being questioned by militia. In all the confusion, we get past the distracted gate-checkers and onto the plane.

Maleeva later gets a call that Danisa has been detained at the airport on the basis of his earlier APB about her. He goes to the airport and it's Hannah, who says she was there to see someone else off, and nobody asked her who she was. At the same moment comes a beeper call that Wechsting and Treacher are raising hell at their hotel, saying they have been robbed of their passports. Maleeva goes there and then begins to tumble, and breaks into Smith's room -- where he finds a tape recorder droning on with the "interview." Maleeva frantically calls his superior, but by that time the flight has landed in Munich and disgorged some of its passengers.

Fjbk, meanwhile, knowing none of this, has begun to figure out that no one can link him to the Chekist's murder. He heads back to work at the arena, figuring everything is going to be all right.

In New York, Partek hears the story of Danisa's defection on his car radio while driving to Chappaqua. Very happy, he dictates some information into a cassette machine and then checks into the inn. Later, Sylvester slips in and kills him.

In Belgrade, very late at night, we find Maleeva in his rooftop apartment where he was seen once before. It's a crummy, lonely place, and he sits on the gravel roof and drinks some beer.

He can't really be sorry Danisa got away. He certainly isn't sorry about Altunyan. No one can prosecute Hannah. Maleeva gets drunk.

On Sunday, I bring Danisa to the county morgue, where her brother's body waits. She weeps and kisses his dead lips. Some Soviets arrive, wanting to claim the body. Danisa says hell no, he is her brother and she is burying him in this country. Dwight and Kinkaid, as well as Collie Davis (who was my original contact in all this), back her up and the Russians leave muttering.

Danisa tells me she will stay, become a citizen, work it out with her family. I offer to help. She accepts, and her love is clear in her eyes.

Dwight tells me that he found a cassette in Partek's car which lists names of many of his operatives in this country. Even in death Partek has given the FBI and CIA priceless information about a massive espionage operation in the US.

With Danisa soon to return, Collie Davis gets me aside for a word of brotherly advice, telling me she is too young for me, it will never work out in the longterm because her career is starting and mine is over, etc., etc. Watching Danisa approach down the hall, I thank him for his advice but say I will just go with it and be with her as long as it does last. And Danisa and I walk out together.

INDEX

A

Adult books, 5

Agents. *See also* Proposal
addressing by name, 79, 86
agreements with, 82-83, 86
approaching by phone, 79, 85-86
commissions and fees of, 78-79,
79-80, 83, 84, 85-86, 87
desirable qualities of , 22-23
directories including, 26, 26-27,
43
vs. editors, 18-21
foreign, 26-27, 43, 80-81, 82, 85
and novels, 18-20
post-agreement information for,
84, 87
querying, 79, 84, 85, 86, 87, 126,
127
questions to ask, 82
responses from, 79, 81-82
searching for, 23-27, 43
and short material, 18
and short story collections, 18
simultaneous submissions to, 80-
81, 85, 86
and subagents, 78, 85
submitting photocopies to, 83-84,
87
types of fiction represented by, 21
types of fiction not represented
by, 21

Anthologies as fiction markets, 10-
11, 17

The Atlantic, 7

Author biography, 88-91, 92-96,
103, 137, 139
with book manuscripts and
proposals, 88, 95, 103
format for, 93, 95, 96

pseudonym in, 95
quotes in, 95
sample, 94
third person in, 92-93

B

Biographical dictionaries, 24

Book packagers, 4
approaching unagented, 20
as fiction markets, 9, 17
querying, 130-31

Book publishers as fiction markets,
8, 17

Business letters:
addressing persons in, 63-64, 66,
76
format for, 62-63
samples of, 71, 123, 125, 128-29

C

Category fiction, 5

Children's books/magazines, 5

*Children's Writer's and Illustrator's
Market*, 39, 43

Clothbound, 5

The Complete Book of Scriptwriting 13

Computer disks, submission on, 55

Contacts, 23, 43, 44, 104-112
agents as best, 106
importance of, 104-105
kinds of, 112
people most likely to know, 107
and sale of One to One, 107
strategies for making, 108-109

Contemporary Authors, 108

Contests, fiction, 13-14

Copyright, 55-56

Corrections in manuscript, how to
make, 54-55

Covering letter(s). *See* Cover
    letter(s)
Cover letter(s), 58, 88-91, 121-24,
    131, 136
    accompanying novel proposal,
        136
    author's background in, 88-91
    content of, 122, 124
    definition of, 121
    elements of successful, 131
    purpose of, 121-22
    sample, 123-25

D

Directory of Publishing, 39

E

Editors:
    book, 37-42
    at book packagers, 42, 44
    importance of spelling names of
        correctly, 43
    locating through personal and
        professional contacts, 42-43,
        44
    locating by phone, 39-40, 44
    magazine, 35-36, 44
    market research on, 43-44
    newspaper magazine
        supplement, 36-37, 44
    phone inquiries to, 39-42
    querying, 130-31
    tips on approaching, 75-77
Ellery Queen's Mystery Magazine, 7
Endorsement, 100-103, 136, 139
    definition of, 100-103
    format for, 101
    importance of, 100-101
    sample, 102
    securing, 101, 103
    with short manuscripts, 103
    types of, 101
Essence, 7
Etiquette for making and using,
    110-11

F

Fiction:

magazines that include, 7
magazines of, 4, 7
newspapers that include, 7
publishers of books of, 8
publishing of, 3-4
types of, 3
Fiction International, 4
Fiction writers, resources for, 16-17
Film, TV, radio, video, audio, stage
    as markets for fiction, 12-13,
        17
Foreign markets, submitting to, 36
Format, checklist for, 64-65

G

Galapagos, 6
Genre fiction, 6
    market resources for, 30
Granta, 10

H

The Handmaid's Tale, 6
Harper's, 7
High Times, 7
Horse Illustrated, 7
House, 5
How to Write a Play, 12

I

Illustrated books, 9-10
*International Directory of Little
    Magazines and Small Presses*, 39
International Literary Market Place, 39
International Reply Coupons, 59,
    60, 68, 80
*International Writer's and Artist's
    Yearbook*, 39

J

Juvenile books/magazines, 5

L

Letter-quality printers and
    typewriters, 46, 63, 64
Library Journal, 31
*Literary Agents: How to Get and Work
    with the Right One for You*, 86
Literary Agents of North America, 43

Literary magazine press, 5
Literary Market Place, 33, 37-39, 42, 43, 44
Little magazine, 6

M

The Magazine of Fantasy and Science Fiction, 7
Magazines as fiction markets, 7, 17
Mainstream, 6
Manuscript. *See also* Response to manuscript submission; Manuscript submissions; Simultaneous submissions
    mailing, 58-61
    packaging, 56-57
    and social security number, 56
Manuscript format, 45-58
    cover page in, 53-54
    first page in, 51-53
    samples of, 47-50
    for series, 57
    tips on, 55-58
    type sizes in, 51
Manuscript submissions. *See also under* Author biography; Endorsement; Writing samples
Market notices vs. sample copies, 34
Market research:
    directories in, 28
    library in, 31-32, 33
    newsstand or bookstore in, 32, 33
    publishers' catalogs in, 32-33
    resources for, for fiction writers, 28-31
    and sample copies from publishers, 33-34
    steps involved in, 27
Markets. *See also* Fiction; *See also under individual types*
    creating your own fiction, 13
    domestic, 2
    fiction, 2-17
    foreign, 2
    list of, 28-30
Masthead, 34, 36-37

lack of, in *The New Yorker*, 35-36
Middle readers, 6
Modern Short Stories, 4
Multiple manuscripts, 73-75. *See also under* Agents
    and series, 74-75
    situations for submitting, 74
Murder at the War, 127

N

New Directions series, 10
Newsletters as fiction markets, 12
Newspapers as fiction markets, 7, 17
The New Yorker, 7, 35, 36
Novel and Short Story Writer's Market, 39, 43
Novella:
    as fiction market, 11
    format of, and ways to market, 55
Novels, excerpted, serialized, and condensed, as fiction markets, 11-12

O

One to One, 107
Organizational affiliations, listing on manuscripts, 91-92, 103
Outline, 113
Outline, novel, 133-35, 141
    Cast of Characters page in, 134, 135, 141
    definition of, 132
    following, in writing of novel, 134-35, 135
    format for, 133, 134, 135
    length of, 134
    person in, 132, 135
    sample excerpt from, 133
    tense in, 132, 135

P

Persistence, 75
Photocopies, 65
    and corrections, 54
    of illustrations, 57
    and submission, 55
The Playwright's Handbook, 12
Plot Synopsis. *See* Outline, novel

Poets & Writers, Inc., 24
Portion and outline. *See* Proposals, novel
Prisoners of Paradise, 116, 134
    outline for, 140-150
Professional Etiquette for Writers, 45
Proposal. *See also* Author biography; Endorsement; Organizational affiliations, listing on manuscript; Reviews; Writing samples
    advances resulting from, 118-19
    advantages of, 113-14
    assembling, 136-39
    author biography in, 88-91
    components of, 113, 136-38, 139
    contracts resulting from, 118-119
    drawbacks of, 114
    vs. entire manuscript, 114-18, 119
    format for, 136-38
    requests from agents for, 81, 83-84
    and sale of *Prisoners of Paradise*, 116
    sample chapters in, 117-18, 137
Publishers, directories of, 25
Publishers Catalogs Annual, 32
Publishers Weekly, 25, 28, 31, 33, 37, 43
    and special issues of, 31
Publishing house, 6

Q

The Quarterly, 10
Query. *See* Query letter
Query letter. *See also* Organizational affiliations, listing on manuscripts
    author's background in, 88-91, 103
    avoiding, with fiction manuscripts, 66-68, 76, 124
    content of, 126-27
    definition of, 121
    elements of successful, 131
    guidelines for writing, 124-30
    project description in, 126-30
    sample, 125, 128-29
    variations on, 127, 130

R

Reader's Digest, 12
Reading fee, 76, 79-80
Records of submissions, 76, 77
Response to manuscript submission, 61-62, 65
Reviews, 97-100, 136, 139
    sample, 99
    submitting with books or proposals, 98, 103
    ways to present, 97-98

S

SASE, 58
The Saturday Evening Post, 7
School Library Journal, 31
The Screenwriter's Handbook, 12
Senior Life, 7
Simultaneous submissions, 69-73
    when to avoid sending, 72-73
    and option clause, 73
    to successor at same publication, 73
Small press, 6
Small publishers, approaching unagented, 20
Something About the Author, 108
Spec sheets. *See* writers' guidelines
Stationery, 63
Stories, 4
Story, 4
Story Quarterly, 4
Subsidy publishing:
    editors' view of, 15
    vs. vanity publishing, 15

T

Telephone correspondence, 64, 65
Television Writer's Handbook, 12
Television Writing—From Concept to Contract, 12
Three Genres, 13
Tiebreaker, 132, 134, 135
    outline for, 151-58
Trade paperbacks, 6

U

Uncertainty of publishing, 16
Universe series, 10

V

Vanity publishing, 14-15
   cost of, 14
   editors' view of, 14-15
   quality of books in, 14

W

Withdrawal letter, 69-70
   sample of, 71
The Writer's Digest Guide to
   Manuscript Formats, 45

The Writer's Directory, 108
Writers' guidelines, 68-69
   how to request, 68
Writer's Market, 26, 28, 39, 43, 86
Writing samples, 96-97, 103, 136,
   139
   with book manuscripts and book
      proposals, 96, 97, 103
   length of, 96-97
   photocopying from published
      work, 96
   submitting to agents, 97

Y

Young adults, 6

Other Books of Interest

Annual Market Books

Artist's Market, edited by Susan Conner $19.95

Children's Writer's & Illustrator's Market, edited by Connie Eidenier (paper) $14.95

Novel & Short Story Writer's Market, edited by Laurie Henry (paper) $17.95

Photographer's Market, edited by Sam Marshall $19.95

Poet's Market, by Judson Jerome $18.95

Songwriter's Market, edited by Mark Garvey $18.95

Writer's Market, edited by Glenda Neff $23.95

General Writing Books

Annable's Treasury of Literary Teasers, by H.D. Annable (paper) $10.95

Discovering the Writer Within, by Bruce Ballenger & Barry Lane $16.95

A Handbook of Problem Words & Phrases, by Morton S. Freeman $16.95

How to Increase Your Word Power, by the editors of Reader's Digest $19.95

How to Write a Book Proposal, by Michael Larsen $10.95

Just Open a Vein, edited by William Brohaugh $15.95

Knowing Where to Look: The Ultimate Guide to Research, by Lois Horowitz (paper) $15.95

Make Every Word Count, by Gary Provost (paper) $9.95

On Being a Writer, edited by Bill Strickland $19.95

The Story Behind the Word, by Morton S. Freeman (paper) $9.95

12 Keys to Writing Books that Sell, by Kathleen Krull (paper) $12.95

The 29 Most Common Writing Mistakes & How to Avoid Them, by Judy Delton $9.95

Word Processing Secrets for Writers, by Michael A. Banks & Ansen Dibell (paper) $14.95

Writer's Block & How to Use It, by Victoria Nelson $14.95

The Writer's Digest Guide to Manuscript Formats, by Buchman & Groves $16.95

Writer's Encyclopedia, edited by Kirk Polking (paper) $16.95

Nonfiction Writing

Basic Magazine Writing, by Barbara Kevles $16.95

How to Sell Every Magazine Article You Write, by Lisa Collier Cool (paper) $11.95

The Writer's Digest Handbook of Magazine Article Writing, edited by Jean M. Fredette $15.95

Writing Creative Nonfiction, by Theodore A. Rees Cheney $15.95

Writing Nonfiction that Sells, by Samm Sinclair Baker $14.95

Fiction Writing

The Art & Craft of Novel Writing, by Oakley Hall $16.95

Best Stories from New Writers, edited by Linda Sanders $16.95

Characters & Viewpoint, by Orson Scott Card $13.95

Creating Short Fiction, by Damon Knight (paper) $9.95

Dare to Be a Great Writer: 329 Keys to Powerful Fiction, by Leonard Bishop $15.95

Dialogue, by Lewis Turco $12.95

Fiction is Folks: How to Create Unforgettable Characters, by Robert Newton Peck (paper) $8.95

Handbook of Short Story Writing: Vol. I, by Dickson and Smythe (paper) $9.95

Handbook of Short Story Writing: Vol. II, edited by Jean M. Fredette $15.95

One Great Way to Write Short Stories, by Ben Nyberg $14.95
Plot, by Ansen Dibell $13.95
Revision, by Kit Reed $13.95
Spider Spin Me a Web: Lawrence Block on Writing Fiction, by Lawrence Block $16.95
Storycrafting, by Paul Darcy Boles (paper) $10.95
Writing the Novel: From Plot to Print, by Lawrence Block (paper) $9.95

Special Interest Writing Books

The Children's Picture Book: How to Write It, How to Sell It, by Ellen E.M. Roberts (paper) $16.95
Comedy Writing Secrets, by Melvin Helitzer $18.95
The Complete Book of Scriptwriting, by J. Michael Straczynski (paper) $11.95
The Craft of Lyric Writing, by Sheila Davis $18.95
Editing Your Newsletter, by Mark Beach (paper) $18.50
Families Writing, by Peter Stillman $15.95
Guide to Greeting Card Writing, edited by Larry Sandman (paper) $9.95
How to Write a Play, by Raymond Hull (paper) $12.95
How to Write Action/Adventure Novels, by Michael Newton $13.95
How to Write & Sell A Column, by Raskin & Males $10.95
How to Write and Sell Your Personal Experiences, by Lois Duncan (paper) $10.95
How to Write Mysteries, by Shannon OCork $13.95
How to Write Romances, by Phyllis Taylor Pianka $13.95
How to Write Tales of Horror, Fantasy & Science Fiction, edited by J.N. Williamson $15.95
How to Write the Story of Your Life, by Frank P. Thomas (paper) $11.95
How to Write Western Novels, by Matt Braun $13.95
Mystery Writer's Handbook, by The Mystery Writers of America (paper) $10.95
The Poet's Handbook, by Judson Jerome (paper) $10.95
Successful Lyric Writing (workbook), by Sheila Davis (paper) $16.95
Successful Scriptwriting, by Jurgen Wolff & Kerry Cox $18.95
Travel Writer's Handbook, by Louise Zobel (paper) $11.95
TV Scriptwriter's Handbook, by Alfred Brenner (paper) $10.95
Writing for Children & Teenagers, 3rd Edition, by Lee Wyndham & Arnold Madison (paper) $12.95
Writing Short Stories for Young People, by George Edward Stanley $15.95
Writing the Modern Mystery, by Barbara Norville $15.95
Writing to Inspire, edited by William Gentz (paper) $14.95

The Writing Business

A Beginner's Guide to Getting Published, edited by Kirk Polking $11.95
The Complete Guide to Self-Publishing, by Tom & Marilyn Ross (paper) $16.95
How to Sell & Re-Sell Your Writing, by Duane Newcomb $11.95
Is There a Speech Inside You?, by Don Aslett (paper) $9.95
Literary Agents: How to Get & Work with the Right One for You, by Michael Larsen $9.95
Professional Etiquette for Writers, by William Brohaugh $9.95
Time Management for Writers, by Ted Schwarz $10.95
The Writer's Friendly Legal Guide, edited by Kirk Polking $16.95
A Writer's Guide to Contract Negotiations, by Richard Balkin (paper) $11.95

To order directly from the publisher, include $3.00 postage and handling for 1 book and 50¢ for each additional book. Allow 30 days for delivery.

Writer's Digest Books
1507 Dana Avenue, Cincinnati, Ohio 45207
Credit card orders call TOLL-FREE
1-800-289-0963
Prices subject to change without notice.

Write to this same address for information on *Writer's Digest* magazine, Writer's Digest Book Club, Writer's Digest School, and Writer's Digest Criticism Service.